HOW TO
THRIVE
IN THE LAST
DAYS

HOW TO THRIVE IN THE LAST DAYS

FRONTLINE

Most CHARISMA HOUSE BOOK GROUP products are available at special quantity discounts for bulk purchase for sales promotions, premiums, fund-raising, and educational needs. For details, write Charisma House Book Group, 600 Rinehart Road, Lake Mary, Florida 32746, or telephone (407) 333-0600.

How to Thrive in the Last Days edited by FrontLine
Published by FrontLine
Charisma Media/Charisma House Book Group
600 Rinehart Road
Lake Mary, Florida 32746
www.charismahouse.com

Copyright © 2015 by FrontLine
All rights reserved

Cover design by Vincent Pirozzi
Design Director: Justin Evans

Visit the publisher's website at www.charismahouse.com.

Library of Congress Cataloging-in-Publication Data:
How to thrive in the last days.
    pages cm
Includes bibliographical references.
ISBN 978-1-62998-206-9 (trade paper) -- ISBN 978-1-62998-257-1 (e-book)
1. Success--Religious aspects--Christianity. 2. Fear--Religious aspects--Christianity.
BV4598.3.H695 2015
248.4--dc23
                                        2015008882

Portions of this book were previously published by Charisma House Book Group as *Recession-Proof Living* by Bill Wiese, ISBN 978-1-61638-478-4, copyright © 2011; *Money Won't Make You Rich* by Sunday Adelaja, ISBN 978-1-59979-458-7, copyright © 2009; *From Boom to Bust and Beyond* by Jerry Tuma, ISBN 978-1-59979-917-9, copyright © 2009; *Financial Boot Camp* by James Paris, ISBN 0-88419-325-X, copyright © 1996; *Financial CPR* by James Paris and J. W. Dicks, ISBN 0-88419-335-7, copyright © 1996; *Breaking the Spirit of Poverty* by Ed Montgomery, ISBN 0-88419-549-X, copyright © 1996. *Earth's Final Moments* by John Hagee, ISBN 978-1-61638-487-6, copyright © 2011. *Prayers That Activate Blessings* by John Eckhardt, ISBN 978-1-61638-370-1, copyright © 2011.

15 16 17 18 19 — 9 8 7 6 5 4 3 2 1
Printed in the United States of America

TABLE OF CONTENTS

AVOIDING FEAR

Today's ever-present threats of terrorist attacks, cataclysmic storms, upheaval in worldwide financial and commodities markets, and threats to Israel's sovereignty have sparked renewed predictions that we are living in the end of time. The apocalyptic atmosphere has prompted numerous predictions of imminent financial collapse and warnings of the need to stockpile supplies. Many live in fear of not having enough or losing everything when end-times prophecies come to pass.

Yet God's people need not live in a state of paralysis, wondering how they can survive uncertainty and upheaval. This book will show you ways of finding hope and safety in God's promises. You will learn practical and biblical ways to protect your finances and experience abundance in times of scarcity. You will learn that money is only one of many signs of wealth, and that we serve a God of limitless abundance and provision. Among its many lessons regarding prosperity are:

- × The need to combine hard work with biblical insights.

- × Why you should save a percentage of your income instead of spending it all.

- × The wisdom of living beneath your means.

- × What Proverbs 13:24 means when it says the wealth of the sinner is stored up for the righteous (and how this reference is usually misinterpreted).

× The need to be a blessing to others, not just a channel of receiving.

How to Thrive in the Last Days aims to equip you to move forward amid the uncertainty and chaos affecting the world. Indeed, if you wisely discern the times, prepare for the future, and embrace God's Word and Spirit, you can move forward with confidence and His peace. Believers have access to every promise and provision God delivered in the Abrahamic covenant. Just as God once prophesied to Israel that they would prosper even in Babylon, believers can claim that promise for today.

Within these pages various financial advisers, business leaders, and spiritual leaders review the insights that God has given them. Their teachings provide a unique combination of prophecy and observations on current events with Bible promises and biblical lessons on wisdom, stewardship, and faithfulness. You will also learn how to break the spirit of poverty and find scripturally based prayers and declarations for provision, increase, blessing, and favor.

In the end you will learn how to face an uncertain future with faith instead of fear.

CHAPTER 1

FINANCIAL FALLACIES THAT RULE THE WORLD

By Jerry Tuma

IMAGINE THE WORLD *without children.* Hard, isn't it? No playgrounds filled with joy and laughter, children running about, being watched by teachers and parents. Doesn't sound much like a fun place, does it?

The world certainly is not in a situation where there are no children. However, many Western societies and others in the developing world have adopted an unbiblical worldview toward global overpopulation concerns. As a result, they have looked on children as a burden, rather than the traditional affirmation of children as a blessing. They don't see the biblical truth that the more children you have, the more blessings they tend to produce.

Beginning in the late 1960s—armed with studies of world deprivation, starvation, shortage, and lack—philosophers, academics, and media moguls altered our view of society and the world. This was due, in part, to the entry of the largest generation in the history of the United States. Namely, the seventy-six million baby boomers born between 1946 and 1964 who entered the economy and workforce. Although viewed through lenses of permanent shortage and lack, these later proved to be temporary shortages caused by this enormous bulge. Yet projected shortages drew doom-and-gloom prognoses from an array of sources and captured the minds of elite academicians and media observers here and across the world.

MALTHUSIAN THINKING

This type of thinking originated more than a century earlier, led by an English economist and demographer named Thomas Robert Malthus (1766–1834). He expressed views on population growth and noted the potential for populations to increase rapidly, often faster than the food supply available to them—a phenomenon known as a *Malthusian catastrophe*, described fully in his *Essay on the Principle of Population*.[1]

Malthus believed that the world's food supplies would only increase arithmetically (1, 2, 3, 4, 5), while population would grow geometrically (1, 2, 4, 8, 16). He felt this would doom large portions of mankind to lives of suffering, deprivation, death, and disease, and that a lack of resources (including food) would always imperil mankind.

Malthus obviously underestimated society's ability to grow without limits. Thus far his theory has proven unfounded. Massive global food shortages and starvation on a grand scale have not occurred. The starvation periods of recent years in sub-Saharan Africa were largely the result of poor economic planning, drought, corruption, and genocide. Given adequate economic resources, the world can support its present population with adequate food.

As proof of this, consider that today food is cheaper and more abundant than ever, even if many still go hungry. Indeed, according to the World Bank, the price of food (adjusted for inflation) declined by 53 percent between 1980 and 2001. The amount of food calories available per person has increased some 20 percent since the 1960s, even as fewer people work as farmers. The

United Nations reports that "the most rapid increase has been in developing countries where population more than doubled and daily food calories available per person rose from roughly 1,900 to 2,600 calories."[2]

Food shortage issues have cropped up globally in recent years. More Malthusian catastrophe? Mankind outgrowing its limits again? Or the result of *human* behavior? In my opinion it's the latter. Millions of acres of land have been converted to grow corn or sugarcane for ethanol production, as shown by the 10 percent increase in farm acres devoted to corn planting the first decade of this century.[3] According to an article in *Science Daily*, "Such conversions for corn or sugarcane (ethanol)...release 17 to 420 times more carbon than the annual savings from replacing fossil fuels."[4]

So we watch the conversion of millions of tons of corn into gasoline—*enough to feed millions of people*—despite the fact that you need 1.5 gallons of ethanol to drive the same distance you go on a gallon of gasoline.[5]

In addition, corn uses more fertilizers and pesticides per unit of land than any other biofuel feedstock. Until the carbon debt is repaid, biofuels produced on converted lands actually emit more carbon than the fossil fuels they replace.[6] Researchers at Princeton University have estimated that it will take roughly 167 years to work off the carbon load placed into the atmosphere given off because of chemical pesticides used in the production of the corn used to produce the ethanol—in order to "save the planet."[7] This boondoggle belongs in the law of unintended consequences Hall of Fame.

Second, China and India's emergence as first-world economies (China in particular, as India is about fifteen years behind them) has radically altered the food supply balance. For more than two decades China has seen millions of rural workers move to cities. These migrants now work in factories instead of on rural farms. This floating population of migrant workers increased an estimated five million per year, reaching 160 million by 2010.[8]

So, first, these workers don't produce food anymore. Second, as city dwellers they must buy their food. Over a decade five or ten million people converting from farming to food-buying annually make a notable difference in the global food supply balance. In addition, as people become more affluent, they tend to consume more meat. Along with rising incomes, the average Chinese citizen's meat consumption, primarily pork, rose 45 percent between 1993–2005.[9]

What does this have to do with food shortages? On average it takes five times more grain in terms of calories consumed to feed a pig than to consume the grain ourselves.[10] Thus, the more meat people eat, the less efficiently we use our resources. (Estimates run as high as ten times the caloric consumption for grain-fed US beef.) A smaller-scale but similar situation is developing in India as they progress in globalization.[11]

So does this mean that the world is running out of scarce resources again? No, it means that humans have changed their behavior on a grand scale and farming has yet to catch up. But it will. These things are cyclical. Despite the hand-wringing over global food supplies—and it's a lot more than just hand-wringing to the poorest of the poor—the resultant food issues are primarily driven by human behavior, not Malthusian limitations.

It appears food shortages in the near future will not be the result of mankind being unable to feed and keep up with its population, but rather of poor economic and political planning, combined with natural events and/or war. A state of permanent food deprivation due to overpopulation cannot be supported by data, only by opinion. Malthusian-type projections and studies by such notable groups as the Club of Rome—a global think tank dealing with various international political issues—projected that by 2000 the world would enter a period of massive starvation, where as much as a third of the world would die from malnutrition, starvation, or disease. Widely disseminated through the media, these projections began to dominate the thinking processes of many Americans.

There are many prophetic signs in Scripture that describe the world in the last days. When all of these ten prophetic signs begin to occur in one generation, that generation will see the end of the age.

1. The knowledge explosion—Daniel 12:4.
2. Plague in the Middle East—Zechariah 14:12–15.
3. The rebirth of Israel—Isaiah 66:8–10.
4. The Jews will return home—Jeremiah 23:7–8.
5. Jerusalem no longer under Gentile control—Luke 21:24.
6. International and instant communication—Revelation 11:3, 7–10.
7. Days of deception—Matthew 24:4.
8. Famines and pestilence—Matthew 24:7–8.
9. Earthquakes—Matthew 24:7–8.
10. "As in the days of Noah..." Matthew 24:36–39.

As you review, research, and meditate on this list, consider carefully the climate and circumstances of this present age.

—JOHN HAGEE, *Earth's Final Moments*

Founded in 1968, this think tank quickly gained public attention with its report *Limits to Growth*. Since its publication in 1972 it has sold thirty million copies in more than thirty translations, making it the world's best-selling environmental book.[12] To this day Malthusian thinking suffuses the environmental movement and casually informs most people's thoughts about the future. But if Malthus was right about the factors that limited human population growth before his time, he was exactly wrong about what the next two centuries would bring. Since he wrote his book, human population has increased more than sixfold, and the amount each person consumes has increased at a more rapid pace.

Instead of widespread famine came a still-expanding system of mass production and mass consumption. Within the United States the population was 3.6 times greater at the end of the twentieth century than at the beginning. Yet living standards are estimated to have increased between fourteen and twenty-five times.[13]

PAUL EHRLICH

Next came Paul Ehrlich's best seller *The Population Bomb*, which not only misled an entire generation but also lives on in the form of extreme environmentalism.[14] The book is primarily a repetition of Malthus's theory of exponential population growth while available resources, especially food, are at their limits. Ehrlich, a biology professor with a background in insect biology, is hardly an expert in demography or population trends. While thoroughly discredited in my opinion, his ideas dominate the thinking of most in the environmental movement and "liberal" agendas. As one example, Ehrlich predicted the US population would fall to twenty-two million by 2000 due to famine and mass starvation. He only missed by some 270 million!

While I'm certainly not in favor of pollution, we must *steward* the world's resources while focusing on long-term growth and prosperity. We must not become myopic about one particular facet of economic development. To ignore or retard longer-term trends of human progress and advancement in order to micro-manage environmental issues is a losing cause. We must take care of the planet (it's the only one we have) but do so with prudence and factual data, not wild conjecture and projections of imminent disaster based on faulty research.

Ehrlich's *The Population Bomb* (along with other parallel thinking) convinced many in this country, especially intellectuals, academics, and the media, that the world faced a certain future of starvation and deprivation. Thus, in order to survive, we had to control world population and work to reduce the number of people, or at least slow the rate of growth. Shortage and permanent "lack" thinking proved fleeting in terms of its economic impact in the 1980s and 1990s. We did see shortages in the 1970s. But again this temporary phenomenon stemmed not from a permanent lack of resources but a society failing to anticipate how immensely the enormous wave of children born after World War II would impact our society.

Shortages began as early as the late 1950s, starting with diapers, baby food, and elementary schools. One demographer, David Cork, referred to this as the "pig in the python" bulge of baby boomers that moved through every element of society.[15] All of this brought radical change. Every place the boomers landed, they created shortages.

1970S STAGFLATION

Thus, shortages abounded, primarily because of the lack of capacity to sustain the enormous bulge of boomers' needs. By the 1980s most of corporate America had caught on to the fact that this enormous group of people was affecting every element of life. However, rather than creating world deprivation, lack, disease, and famine, this generation launched an unprecedented period of economic growth and prosperity.

As an example, in 1980 the Dow Jones Industrial Average was under 1,000, where it had languished for almost fourteen years due to stagflation caused largely by poorer demographics and Keynesian economic policies of excessive government control, regulation, and taxation. (See Chart 1-A.)

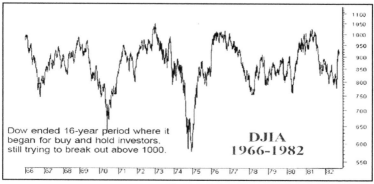

Dow ended 16-year period where it began for buy and hold investors, still trying to break out above 1000.

DJIA
1966-1982

Chart 1-A

This period of stagflation (economic stagnation plus inflation) largely originated with two economic forces. The first was demographics. Economic growth is dependent upon consumer spending. The more consumers you have entering their peak-spending mode (ages forty-five to fifty), the stronger the economy. The 1970s saw a drop in consumer spending because of a plummeting birth rate in the Great Depression of the 1930s.[16]

That meant a small group of Americans were propelling the economy several decades later. If you take the year 1930, then add forty-five years to it to project peak family spending for that age group, you get 1975. Thus, part of the 1970s economic malaise came from low Depression-era births.

The second factor that increased the misery of the 1970s was political and economic in origin. Lyndon B. Johnson's guns-and-butter Vietnam acceleration, plus social spending (the Great Society—in which the government added more to programs that began in the 1930s—created unprecedented rates of inflation. Government spending ratcheted out of control.[17] Later came the Carter years, which took micromanaging the economy to an all-new level. During the 1970s terms such as *stagflation* and the *misery index* (inflation plus unemployment) arose. All in all the 1970s was largely a miserable decade.

REAGAN PLUS BOOMERS EQUALS PROSPERITY

However, around the time Ronald Reagan became president, the unprecedented baby boom generation had already entered the workforce, with the tail end of this demographic group nearing college age. Starting with minimal impact at first, boomers began having families, buying houses, and pushing both the economy and the stock market higher.

Before the final wave of economic boomer influence reached its apex in 2007, the Dow hit 14,000. (See Chart 1-B.) That's an increase of 1,727 percent in the most widely watched stock index in the world.

People earned massive fortunes during this time. As a matter of fact, prior to the late 1980s the term *billionaire* was almost unheard of. Of the thirteen billionaires in the United States prior to 1985, only a few, such as Warren Buffett and Bill Gates, proved noteworthy. By the late 1990s there were more than one thousand billionaires worldwide and dozens of multibillionaires throughout the world.[18]

DOW JONES INDUSTRIAL AVERAGE 1980–2008

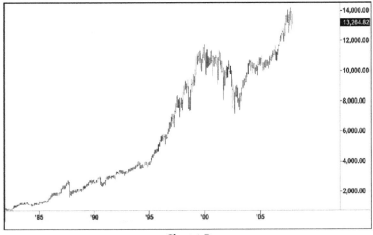

Chart 1-B

The period of prosperity launched in the early 1980s is literally unparalleled in world history. Stop for a moment and ask yourself: What caused this unparalleled growth and unmatched wave of prosperity?

More people bought homes, cars, and clothing during this time than at any other time in world history. As a result, more wealth was created than at any other time in world history. New companies and technologies emerged amid the explosion of the Internet and the telecommunications/technology revolution.

All of these innovations and growth came about largely as the result of one thing—the growth and subsequent prosperity of an enormous group of people, indeed a population boom.

As a matter of fact, if you trace world history (even with sketchy statistics of the past), you will find that there is an immutable link in societies that have dominated throughout world history. For the most part, for advanced countries the larger the population group, the larger the number of people to fill the society and the economy, and the more financially blessed the society.

Obvious modern exceptions would be 1950–1980 communist China under Mao Tse-tung and socialist India from 1950–1991. The reason these societies experienced poverty lay not in their massive populations, but their political and economic systems. Communism and socialism do not work. With the institution of free-market reforms that have taken hold, both of these countries are creating their own economic prosperity.

Over the long run there is irrefutable proof that prosperity generally comes to societies with free trade and large numbers of offspring. This has been the view throughout history until recent decades.

Think about it. When seventy-six million people got out of high school and college and moved into the workforce, what did they want? They started by living in apartments and then moved into starter homes. They bought cars, had children, and took those kids to McDonald's. This unprecedented wave of consumer spending launched prosperity that stayed with us for almost three decades.

Like a Hawaiian surfer riding a gigantic wave, a veritable tidal wave of consumer spending from boomers engulfed the entire US and world economy. American investments, stocks, bonds, real estate—every element used to measure wealth and health— rode this *gigantic* wave all the way to the beach.

Current-Dollar and "Real" Gross Domestic Product[19]	
Annual GDP in billions of current dollars	
1980	2,789.5
1981	3,128.4
1982	3,255.0
1983	3,536.7
1984	3,933.2
1985	4,220.3
1986	4,462.8
1987	4,739.5
1988	5,103.8
1989	5,484.4
1990	5,803.1
1991	5,995.9
1992	6,337.7
1993	6,657.4
1994	7,072.2
1995	7,397.7
1996	7,816.9
1997	8,304.3
1998	8,747.0
1999	9,268.4
2000	9,817.0
2001	10,128.0
2002	10,469.6
2003	10,960.8

Current-Dollar and "Real" Gross Domestic Product	
Annual GDP in billions of current dollars	
2004	11,685.9
2005	12,421.9
2006	13,178.4
2007	13,807.5
2008	14,264.6

In the chart of gross domestic product (GDP) growth, note that GDP (before inflation adjustment) rose from 2.7 trillion to 14 trillion as seventy-six million boomers moved into the workforce and began their consumer spending splurge.

BOOMER WAVE HITS THE BEACH

Unfortunately the tide has shifted. The boomer wave has now hit the beach. The monstrous economic growth wave created by the largest consumer group in history had to hit rocky shores. The first wave to strike came in the US housing market. After researching this topic for two decades without finding a painless solution, I strongly believe we have entered an unprecedented "demographic winter," something unknown to the modern world.

This is affecting the United States as well as Japan, western European societies, and other parts of the world that have decided they needed birth control, abortion, and other methods of population reduction. These have become the preferred methods for dealing with and attempting to centrally manage human population needs. (For historical reference, Margaret Sanger and Katherine McCormick submitted the first birth control pill to the Food and Drug Administration in 1956.[20] The *Roe v. Wade* US Supreme Court decision of 1973 legalized abortion.[21])

The lesson here is that central planning by large government institutions has historically been ineffective and often creates unintended pain, usually inflicted by well-meaning politicians.

As a free-market economist, I would submit that the vast

majority of the time, the marketplace is much better at determining what products or services need to be produced, not some
government attempting to control from the top down. The same
is "population control." When the government intervenes, it typically messes things up. As Nobel Prize-winning economist, the
late Milton Friedman, once said, "The government solution to
the problem is usually as bad as the problem."[22]

The point is this: there is no way to alter the number of people
born between 1961 and 1974, when we saw an enormous drop
in birthrates due to such factors as the sexual revolution, more
women entering the work force, abortion, and birth control. My
concern is that we have entered a demographic winter. Over the
next several decades this will have enormous repercussions on
the United States and the entire world.

Economically the United States still dominates the world.
While other countries may resent it, the United States is still the
dominant economy of the world. With less than 5 percent of the
world's population and less than 5 percent of its land mass, this
nation produced nearly one-third of the world's GDP in the year
2000. This means that nearly one-third of the goods and services
produced in the entire world then were produced in the United
States.[23]

Although China is working hard to catch up, the United States
remains the world's proverbial eight-hundred-pound gorilla. Yet I
don't write only for readers in the United States (English speaking
and otherwise) but also to those all over the world for this simple
reason: the direction that the US economy takes in the next decade
will have *massive ramifications* on the world economy, whether
they be Eastern, European, or those in the Middle East.

If September 11, 2001 proved anything, it proved America is
not immune from attack from our enemies. September 11 also
proved, beyond any reasonable doubt, that our enemies are
willing to use whatever weapons they have to kill as many of

us as possible. The highest honor in Islam is to die as a martyr killing Christians and Jews. The one who does this awakes in an Islamic heaven surrounded by seventy-two virgins....No prophetic scripture is more crystal clear than Ezekiel's vivid and specific description of the coming massive war in the Middle East that will sweep the world toward Armageddon. Ezekiel's war as described in chapters 38 and 39 will consist of an Arab coalition of nations led by Russia for the purpose of exterminating the Jews of Israel and controlling the city of Jerusalem. The Russian payout will be the ability to control the oil-rich Persian Gulf.

—JOHN HAGEE, *Earth's Final Moments*

As US boomers continue to age and move further away from peak spending years, this massive population tsunami will literally affect every aspect of American society. The ripples will be felt across the world.

When baby boomers who started hitting Social Security and Medicare systems in 2010 reach critical mass, it will place enormous strains on entitlement and retirement systems. A 2014 government report noted: "Social Security's total expenditures have exceeded non-interest income of its combined trust funds since 2010 and the Trustees estimate that Social Security cost will exceed non-interest income throughout the 75-year projection period."[24]

America is about to embark upon a new journey. We have never seen seventy-six million people, who up until this point had been spending, spending, and spending, thus driving the economy to ever higher heights, regress in spending as they age and move into retirement.

William H. Gross, cofounder of the giant bond investment firm PIMCO, used his own colorful language to describe the recent past—and provide a vision of the future: "U.S. and many global consumers gorged themselves on Big Macs of all varieties: burgers to be sure, but also McHouses, McHummers, and

McFlatscreens, all financed with excessive amounts of McCredit created under the mistaken assumption that the asset prices securitizing them could never go down. What a colossal McStake that turned out to be."[25]

The hit the economy has already experienced in terms of consumer spending will be like nothing ever seen. By 2007 we received all of the benefit of the trend's upside. Now that the wave has reached the beach and is crashing, it will affect every aspect of society. My concern, and the main reason for this message, is helping others to prepare. Not everyone will listen. With their finances, most people react like those following the latest fashions—copying others around them. Whether tuned in to consumer sites, Madison Avenue, or mass media, most Americans spend with little thought for tomorrow. They assume the future will be brighter. For three decades, this type of thinking paid off as we rode wave after wave of prosperity. Despite downturns and bear markets, since the early 1980s, every recession prior to 2007 proved fairly shallow and short, with the exception of the 2000–2003 drop for NASDAQ and the dot-coms.

However, we are facing unprecedented circumstances. The mostly short, shallow downturns occurred during a thirty-year boomer *boom*. The long-term megatrend of boomer spending kept the *busts* short and shallow, with each slowdown followed by another, bigger wave of consumer spending. But this trend is reversing.

THE JAPANESE EXAMPLE

We will never have a perfect economic road map. We will not know for certain exactly how this plays out, but the evidence from previous societies' experience is not encouraging. The best illustration from modern history is Japan, a highly mechanized and technologically sophisticated economy. Yet if you look at Japanese society, they are much older. Unlike Americans, as a defeated nation Japan did not experience a baby boom following

World War II. With Shintoism as their dominant religion, the Japanese were trained from birth that their emperor *was God.*

So their military defeat left a despondent and depressed nation. Not only were they completely disillusioned by the discovery that their emperor was not God, they had two cities lying in nuclear waste. Unlike American GIs, after World War II Japanese soldiers did not go home and celebrate. Everything they had believed proved a lie. As this reality set in, they slowly picked up the pieces and (rather remarkably) rebuilt their lives.

Japan did rebuild phenomenally and became the second-largest economy in the world until China surpassed it in 2010. However, the Japanese population curve looks like ours is about to look—only twenty years in advance. If you look at their spending curve, as a society the Japanese topped out in consumer spending in 1989, *precisely* when both the Japanese stock and real estate markets topped.[26]

You may remember the Japanese buying Pebble Beach golf course, Rockefeller Center in New York, and other notable real estate trophy "assets" in the United States. By the late 1980s many Americans were concerned that the Japanese were going to economically take over the world. (You might remember in one of the movies in the *Back to the Future* trilogy, Michael J. Fox's future boss was Japanese. They had taken over!)

The Japanese real estate market created such an extreme bubble that the Emperor's Palace in Japan and surrounding land was reportedly valued at a price exceeding the value of all real estate in the entire state of California![27]

Though we now know this to be absurd, it demonstrates the height of investment mania. When the Japanese stock market topped out, the Nikkei average hit almost 40,000.[28] At that time the average price/earnings ratio of Japanese stock was at eighty (roughly three times more expensive than comparable major tops in the US market). It was truly a mania—right at the top of their demographic curve. Sound familiar? It should!

Unfortunately, once the balloon expanded to a certain level and burst, there was no way to reinflate their asset values. Japanese stock and real estate could only go one way—down.

After this demographic wave topped out, the Japanese experienced a fourteen-year-long bear market, culminating in 2002 with the Nikkei bottoming out at 7,800, spelling an 80 percent decline for the average Japanese stock.

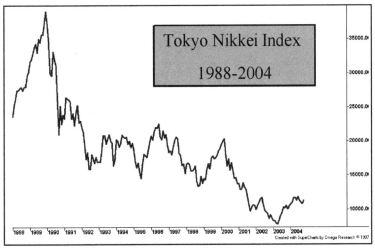

Chart 1-C

I am not attempting to alarm anyone. Like greed-based decisions, those rooted in fear tend to lead to big problems. Still, forewarned is forearmed. We need to make rational, intelligent, well-informed, well-thought-out decisions, not panicky ones. We must come to terms with the facts of current economic reality, which come as a result of being hit broadside unexpectedly by Wall Street's shenanigans, plus a megatop in US housing.

We have no guarantees that the United States will follow the pattern of Japan. Yet, every economic study we can find demonstrates close parallels between consumer spending patterns and overall economic prosperity, or lack thereof.

FAMILY SPENDING AND THE STOCK MARKET

In this section we want to demonstrate that there is a strong correlation between the number of people that hit their peak family spending years and the stock market. As mentioned earlier, peak spending for the average family typically occurs between the ages of forty-five and fifty. Since consumer spending drives the economy, it makes logical sense that the larger the number of people at peak family spending, the stronger the economy. In turn, the stronger the economy, the more corporate earnings will rise, and the stronger the stock market.

Generally defined as births between 1945 and 1965, the baby boom generation makes up nearly eighty million people, or two-thirds of our nation's workforce. As you can see from Chart 1-D, in the late 1960s abortion, birth control, and other actions brought the birthrate in our country way, way down, resulting in a much smaller group of people following the boomers—only forty-one million baby busters.

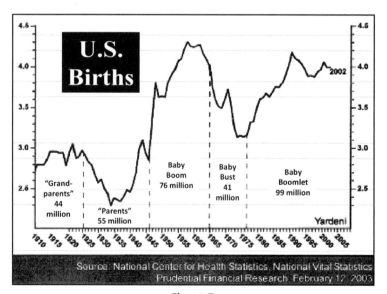

Chart 1-D

The next chart, 1-E, shows the strong relation between the number of people hitting peak spending (births lagged to peak family spending) and the stock market. Note the strong correlation between the number of people hitting their spending peak and the stock market, adjusted for inflation. The final wave of boomers hit their peak spending years between 2003 and 2010, as shown in the chart. Thus, boomers put strong upward momentum behind the economy during the past decade. However, it is likely to weaken radically in the future.

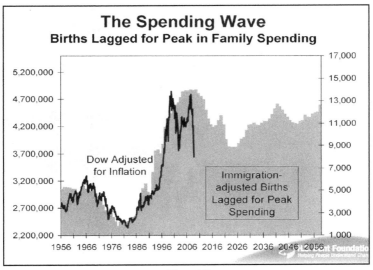

Chart 1-E

Still, if you look at the very long-term history for the market, you will see something similar to the old real estate saying, "Location, location, location." Obviously, location is not the only factor that makes a real estate property successful or not, but it *can be the single most important factor*. The same is true of the stock market regarding earnings. To me, it is almost undeniable that the single most important factor over time is corporate earnings. There tends to be a strong correlation between the health of American corporations, as reflected in corporate earnings and the number of people who are hitting their peak in spending. Notice the long-term correlation between corporate earnings and the S&P 500 in the 1990s in chart 1-F.

Chart 1-F

Now, look again at the birthrate curves (Chart 1-D). Then compare it to 1-E. The second chart simply pushes forward (or lags) the population curve out to *peak family spending*. The baby boomer cycle (which topped in 1961) hit its final peak for consumer spending in late 2009, when the median boomer family hit its overall spending peak.

Just as the average person peaks in consumer spending for housing at around age forty-four, the average individual peaks in consumer spending for most other items around forty-eight years old. Take this a step further, this meant the top of the megatrend for baby boomers positively affecting our economy topped out around 2009. Thus, it is our assertion that housing spending tops first and other spending tops several years later, which we can see in our current crisis.

A question presents itself: If the economic wave that is likely to be produced from China, India, and other developing countries is such a mammoth wave, how can you be sure that it will not completely offset the decline in spending power and economic thrust of the baby boom generation? Here's how.

In 2006 the average per capita income of a Chinese citizen was $2,010 per year. The United States equivalent per capita income for wage earners here was $44,970 per year.[29] Regardless of how many Chinese you have spending, they simply can't offset the boomer spending decrease. It just won't happen fast enough.

Prior to the 2008 meltdown the world had started seeing shortages cropping up almost everywhere—most noticeably in petroleum, steel, concrete, food, and other commodities. At the same time, China was experiencing their version of the Industrial and Technological Revolutions *combined*.

To those Malthusians out there, this (again) is not the end of the world, nor a sign that permanent deprivation is here and that there are not enough resources to go around. This is a *utilization* problem. The world is simply not finding enough of these particular products fast enough to keep pace with the stunning economic growth that has been occurring in these countries and other developing countries around the world.

On the one hand we are seeing the US baby boom generation consumer spending trend ride off into the sunset; on the other hand we are seeing the economic sun rising in the Far East, which will indeed have a phenomenal impact over the long run.

In terms of shortages of raw materials and commodities, what we have seen is similar to what we saw in the United States in the 1970s, when seventy-six million boomers created supply shortages, only on a much larger scale.

Thus, it is going to take a period of dislocation and problem-solving to navigate the world through this. Until we have the capability of getting enough oil, mining, steel, and other raw commodities to supply economic giants developing in the Far East, more inflationary pressure—in terms of commodities and energy—from China and India is coming down the road. While in the short term, the boomers moving toward retirement will create deflationary pressures (think California and Florida real estate), over the long haul, inflation could be our worst enemy.

I am reminded of the old Chinese proverb: "May you live in interesting times." The Chinese character for *crisis* represents both *opportunity* and *danger*. In my view the coming time in America and for the world over the next decade represents both. Many of the greatest potential opportunities of your investment and financial lifetime will likely present themselves. Simultaneously, those years also represent our greatest danger.

Like the old football saying: "Luck is when preparation meets opportunity," there will be unprecedented potential for opportunity for both economic and financial gain. On the other hand, there will be extreme danger too. Looking at recorded history, challenging economic times also present great opportunities, and extremely challenging times present the most rewarding opportunities.

The worst recorded economic scenario of modern world history was the Great Depression of the 1930s. Even in that environment, with unemployment skyrocketing to 25 percent, *there were more millionaires created per capita than in any other time in US history!*[30]

Those who were unprepared in essence lost their assets to others who were either prepared or adapted. I believe that the coming times we face over the next ten years could represent equal opportunity and/or danger to this most amazing period of US history.

I am not predicting an economic depression or anything of the sort. As an investment adviser, I strive diligently not to make predictions, because once you've made a prediction, your ego gets involved and you start focusing on being right rather than being flexible enough to change as the situation changes. What I am saying is that according to everything that I can see on a macro-economic level, the perfect economic storm has just begun. You need to be prepared.

CHAPTER 2

BRACING FOR THE BIG CHILL

By Jerry Tuma

AS MUCH AS I'd like to tell you the financial crisis that began in 2008 is over, I can't. It's far from over! Below is a list of just a few reasons why the bottom appears to be several years away.

1. *Excess inventory of homes*—Estimates of continuing excess housing supply due to "euphoric" investment-oriented housing decisions and foreclosures. In the spring of 2014 the *New York Times* reported that from 2007 to 2013 builders constructed 4.8 million fewer homes than they would have going by normal trends as they struggled to work through an oversupply of 2.1 million homes created during the boom.[1]

   Never before the bubble had Americans considered their homes their best investment. Unfortunately, millions around the country discovered how poor an investment housing amid timing and debt problems. Before the housing market can bottom nationwide, all—repeat, all—of the excess housing inventory must be soaked up, either bought out of foreclosure or dumped through distress sales. Housing prices cannot finally bottom out until supply no longer exceeds demand.

2. *Alt-As just starting to reset*—An Alt-A mortgage refers to "Alternative A" paper, considered risker than A-paper (or prime) and less risky than sub-prime loans; they are often labeled "liar loans." As seen in the following charts, these Alt-A mortgages started to reset at the beginning of the housing crisis and pushed payments for homeowners significantly higher.

   As we saw in round one of the housing bubble, once the subprime interest rate resets hit, defaults began to skyrocket. While homeowners across the nation bought these risky mortgages, the heaviest purchases occurred in bubble states.

3. *Option ARMs*—Option ARMs are another ticking time bomb. Despite the fact that this subset of creative mortgages was numerically smaller than Alt-As, their resets were more devastating, with the average reset going from $1,672 per month to $2,725 per month—*up* 63 percent!

4. *HELOCs (home equity line of credit) and second mortgages*—Home equity lines of credit and second mortgages are 100 percent exposed to loss, as only the primary mortgage holder has rights to foreclose in order to recover some of the losses. Estimates totaled more than $1 trillion in loss exposure to our banking system on these loans, which were issued predominately near the top of the bubble.

5. *Foreclosures/pressure prices*—In recent years home prices continued to fall as foreclosures rose. As

home prices fell, it made it even more difficult for a struggling homeowner, who may have seen his mortgage payment rise dramatically due to the gimmicky mortgage resetting (subprimes, Alt-As, option ARMs). Many chose not to justify this albatross around their necks. Skyrocketing mortgage payments combined with crashing home prices did not make for a quick turnaround or even a short-term bottom.

6. *Strategic defaults.* Many homeowners in bubble areas of the country strategically decided to default on their home mortgages, despite being capable of making the payments.

Strategic default refers to making a decision to walk away from a home that has fallen sharply in value. A 10 percent decline won't do it, but many homeowners were 30 percent or more under water and simply walked away. Research shows that people are more likely to default if they either know someone else who has done it or it has occurred in their neighborhood, despite the fact that most consider it morally wrong.[2] (I guess it's OK if everyone else is doing it, right?)

7. *Job losses in the hardest-hit areas create more downward pressure on home prices*—Job losses continue as rising unemployment forces more foreclosures. Most consumers have lived paycheck-to-paycheck for much of their lives; thus, when one spouse loses a job, foreclosure often is the consequence.

8. *The "worst" mortgages are heavily under water—* The most egregious mortgages are primarily grouped in the bubble states, where home prices have fallen the hardest. These bad mortgage types

put even more pressure on home prices as default piles upon default.

9. *Expected losses are only half realized*—Two years into this debacle, projected losses were less than one-half realized, regardless of the source used to estimate expected losses. The charts that follow make it obvious that the mortgage fiasco's effect upon our economy and its financial system won't end quickly.

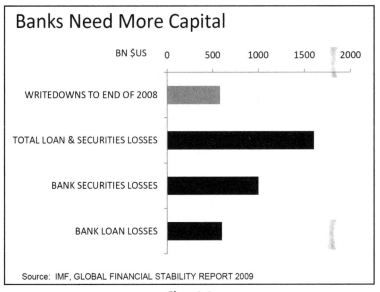

Chart 2-A

What was not widely known is that, back in 2009 while the subprime fiasco still had time to run and defaults continued to climb, parts two and three of the debacle were actually bigger in terms of dollar-loan amounts than subprimes ever thought about being. Fortunately, the vast majority of subprime interest rate resets are behind us, but we are still paying the price for the irrationality of the past. As one report noted, "Reinforced by many years of experience, both lenders and borrowers assumed that home prices would keep rising and easy credit would keep flowing, allowing borrowers to refinance before the reset."[3]

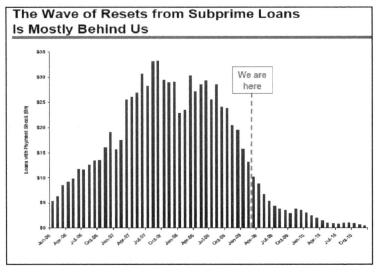

Chart 2-B

Alt-A and option ARM mortgage resets, on the other hand, are still ahead of us and they represent billions more in losses for financial firms. When I first wrote about this in the summer of 2009, it appeared that round one of the "Great Mortgage Rip-off" was drawing to a close. But the problems related to Alt-As and ARMs continued. Both of these recently created mortgages have yet to extract their full measure of pain upon either homeowners or the financial system.

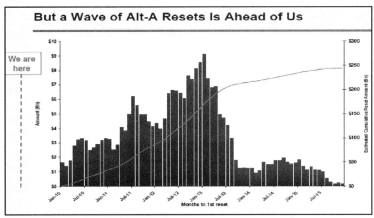

Chart 2-C

A PRIMER ON OPTION ARMS

To help you better understand the problems of adjustable-rate mortgages, here is a brief primer:

1. An option ARM is an adjustable-rate mortgage typically made to a prime borrower.

2. Banks typically relied on the appraised value of the home and the borrower's high FICO score, so 83 percent of the option ARMs written in 2004–2007 were low or no document loans (known as "liar loans").

3. Each month the borrower can choose to pay: (1) the fully amortizing interest and principal; (2) full interest; or (3) an ultra-low teaser interest-only rate (typically 2–3 percent), in which case the unpaid interest is added to the balance of the mortgage (meaning it negatively amortizes). Approximately 80 percent of option ARMs are negatively amortizing. Lenders, however, booked earnings as if the borrowers were making full interest payments.

4. A typical option ARM is a thirty- or forty-year mortgage that resets after five years when it becomes fully amortized. If an option ARM negatively amortizes to 110–125 percent of the original balance (depending on the loan's terms), this triggers a reset, even if five years have not elapsed.

5. Upon reset, the average monthly payment jumps 63 percent from $1,672 to $2,725 (meaning annually total payments jump from $20,064 to $32,700).[4]

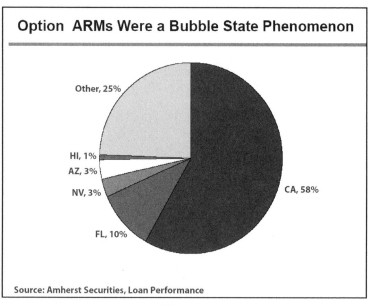

Chart 2-D

HOUSING FACTS

The following facts about the housing market provide further clarification about our current condition:

✗ The mortgage-lending standards that became progressively worse starting in 2000 went off a cliff beginning in early 2005.

✗ It takes an average of fifteen months from the date of the first missed payment by a homeowner to liquidation of the home (generally a sale via auction).

✗ The oversupply left us too much inventory to work off quickly, especially in light of the millions of foreclosures that hit our economy in recent years.

✗ While in recent years foreclosure sales are booming in many areas, regular sales by homeowners plunged. That partially is because people usually can't sell when they owe more on their mortgages than their homes are worth and in part because of human psychology. People naturally anchor on the price they paid or its past value and are reluctant to sell below this level. In 2005, 29 percent of new mortgages were interest-only—or less, in the case of option ARMs—versus the 1 percent level in 2001.

✗ The sale of new homes costing $750,000 or more quadrupled from 2002 to 2006.

✗ In the 2004–2006 time period, between 18–20 percent of all home sales were subprime.

✗ In January 2009 distressed sales accounted for 45 percent of all existing home sales nationwide—and more than 60 percent in California. In addition, the *shadow* inventory that year of foreclosed homes exceeded one year, creating a huge overhang of excess supply. Thus, weak demand was still with us five years later.

× We are also quite certain that wherever prices bottom, there will be no quick rebound.

× Given that lending standards got much worse in late 2005 through 2006 and into the first half of 2007, and that many other types of loans with longer reset dates then started to default at catastrophic rates, we were left sobering implications for expected defaults, foreclosures, and auctions well beyond 2009.

× More mortgage meltdown:

  × 10 percent of homes built during the first decade of this century were vacant at its end.

  × 29 percent of loans made in the last half of that decade were under water by its end.[5]

Hopefully, these issues will be handled better next time, but forewarned is forearmed; and, personally, I'd rather be safe than sorry at this point. So, while defaults on subprimes are still escalating, clearly the reset trend—which is ultimately the primary reason for the defaults anyway—is mostly behind us.

Alt-As and option ARM resets were just starting to happen as the nation reeled from 2008's collapse. Historically, bubbles of this type have taken about six years (or longer) to unwind for housing, as opposed to around three years for stock bubbles. Because stocks are more liquid and easily traded, their bubbles unwind much faster than less liquid real estate, which takes much longer to go through the foreclosure/sales process.

AFTERMATH OF A "TYPICAL" FINANCIAL CRISIS

The aftermath of a financial crisis usually includes the following factors:

✗ *Housing*—six-year adjustment

✗ *Unemployment*—rises 7 percent (11–12 percent).

✗ *Stocks*—3.5-year bear market.

✗ *Real GDP*—down 9 or more percent.[6]

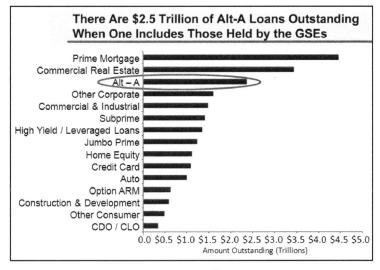

Chart 2-E[7]

With more than $3 trillion worth of potential losses in Alt-As and option ARMs at risk, falling real estate prices plus rapidly escalating mortgage payments virtually guarantee more pain to come. In spite of authorities' best efforts, more real estate and economic pain lies ahead.

How, you ask, might this affect others not in the bubble states, as well as other financial assets, such as stocks?

First, non-bubble states will obviously still be affected, likely to a lesser degree but, in some cases, to a much less degree. It is reminiscent of the dot-com era, when the average dot-com fell 90 percent and the average tech stock fell 80 percent (the NASDAQ fell 78 percent from top to bottom), but the Dow Jones Industrial

Average—full of mostly the blue-chip stocks—fell just 37 percent. A 37 percent drop still hurts but is not an irreversible, catastrophic loss (like the dot-coms).

Bubble real estate is not likely to fall 90 percent, as the dot-coms were mostly just hype and hope—a lot of hot air waiting to burst. Real estate in San Diego or Las Vegas, while it certainly has tangible value (unlike most dot-coms), still became tremendously overvalued. A 70 percent drop or more is entirely possible, given the fact that many of these areas are already down 50 percent or so, with more mortgage problems on the way.

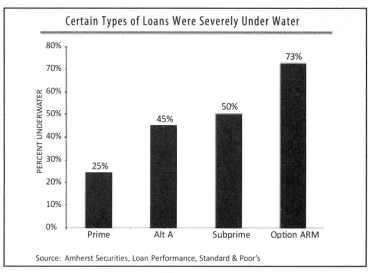

Chart 2-F

Thus, the greatest mortgage fiasco in our country's history, brought on by the largest population group in our country's history, lingers.

FROM WALL STREET TO MAIN STREET

Once the housing debacle hit Wall Street, it then spread to Main Street as consumers, panicked at seeing their 401(k)s plummet while large numbers of major financial institutions went bankrupt almost on a moment-by-moment basis, immediately clamped down on their purse strings.

Jesus presented a portrait of the end of the age and the coming of the Messiah. He presents a series of signs, including international wars, famines, and earthquakes. He makes a profound statement: "All these are the beginning of birth pains" (Matt. 24:8, NIV). There are two facts about a woman in labor about to have a child. First, when the birth pains start, they do not stop until the child is born. Second, the birth pains become more severe and more rapid as birth approaches.

The last pain is the greatest pain, and it is soon forgotten with the birth of the new child. The world and Israel are now having contractions (wars, rumors of wars, acts of terrorism, bloodshed, and violence around the globe) that will produce a new Messianic era. The increasing rapidity and intensifying of these birth pains can be seen on the newscasts every evening. We are racing toward the end of the age.

—JOHN HAGEE, *Earth's Final Moments*

Remember that consumer spending is what drives the economy, and consumer spending went from high gear into reverse in a matter of sixty days. This, combined with the freezing up of the credit markets, had a domino effect that spread worldwide.

In Chart 2-G you can see that global shipping literally fell almost to zero in a matter of less than six months. The cost of renting one of the world's largest freight ships dropped from $132,000 per day *to $2,700 a day*, representing an *unprecedented 94 percent decline* in shipping costs virtually overnight!

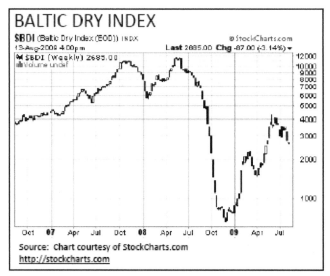

BALTIC DRY INDEX

$BDI (Baltic Dry Index (EOD)) INDX
13-Aug-2009 4:00 pm   © StockCharts.com
                          Last 2685.00 Chg -87.00 (-3.14%) ▼
W $BDI (Weekly) 2685.00
Volume undef

Source: Chart courtesy of StockCharts.com
http://stockcharts.com

Note: This index shows the incredible drop in global
shipping, which has recovered (according to this shipping
cost index) approximately one-third from the high.

Chart 2-G

This was such a blind side to the economy, but the magnitude
of these losses in the financial system was completely hidden
from consumers; all the while, authorities continued to reas-
sure us that all was well. As a result, corporations were totally
unprepared for the incredible drop in sales. Unsold inventories
surged, and the only way to get rid of these inventories was to
slash prices, as shown in Chart 2-H.

Chart 2-H

With US retail prices slashed throughout America, we entered into the world of a central banker's worst nightmare: a *deflationary* environment.

In such an environment prices fall due to lack of orders. But that's not the worst. Deflationary behavior tends to reinforce itself, thus becoming a *self-reinforcing process*. What do I mean by this?

In deflation prices begin falling and consumers learn to anticipate that prices will be lower next year—or a few months down the road. So they decide to postpone new purchases, which creates additional excess inventories for businesses to have to liquidate. Again, the only way to liquidate inventories is to reduce the prices. Consumers then say, "Aha, I knew if I waited longer the price would go down." This reinforces their beliefs, meaning more delays that exacerbate the problem. The cycle repeats itself, and the longer the process runs, the more difficult it is to break.

Over the past century we've seen two cases of deflation. The first came in the 1930s, when the United States faced a *severe* deflation, which bottomed out in three and a half years. The second: Japan's deflationary spiral that began in 1990. It appears that the spiral continued for twenty years, but in reality may not yet be over.[8]

In our current crisis the problem we have is that at the precise top of the demographic megatrend, Wall Street, the banks, and investment bankers all went on a wild mortgage-lending spree. Like a bunch of drunken sailors with pockets full of money, they nearly blew up the system, almost exactly at the top of our demographic curve.

Thus, what we have faced in recent years is not an ordinary, garden-variety recession.

It will play out nothing like past recessions. Recent recessions occurred in the context of a thirty-year baby boomer-induced boom. Now we are in the mid-phase of a ten- or fifteen-year *baby boomer bust*. This recession will cut deeper and last longer than any in recent history and has the potential to become a depression before it is over.

During the boom, banks grossly over-lent, and now that the horse is out of the barn, they have shut the door. Although consumers went on a borrowing binge like none in history, they are now feeling a lot less rich than they were before. Making it worse, the biggest wave of boomers is not far from retirement, with a much smaller asset base than before.

Thus, we are in a classic scenario economists refer to as "pushing on a string." The twenty-five-year borrowing binge is over. Banks don't want to lend, consumers don't want to borrow, and until this has time to wash through the system, it won't turn around quickly.

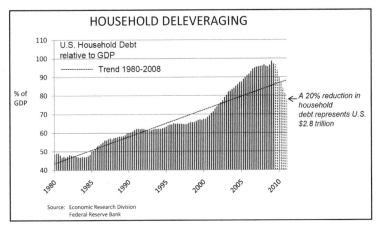

Chart 2-I

Chart 2-I shows projected household deleveraging. The dashed line represents the median of what consumers would be expected to borrow based upon normal times. As you can see, during the housing bubble the average US household went much deeper into debt than ever before. Thus, we had not only a housing bubble but a credit bubble as well.

The problem with this picture is that historically the pendulum of change never stops in the middle; it goes from one extreme to the other. In this case, household borrowing, which ran up to extreme levels during the bubble, is unlikely to stop dropping at the trend line but will likely overshoot on the downside as well. This means extended and painful deleveraging as consumers reduce borrowing and pay down debt, as well as increase their savings.

So, you might ask, what's so bad about that? Consumers increasing their savings and paying down debt would normally be viewed as a positive and will eventually be necessary to get us out of this morass. The problem is *when* it started occurring— just after the 2008 meltdown, amid skyrocketing unemployment, corporations hit hard, and bankruptcies on the rise. This all means it would not end quickly. When we do finally bottom, it is unlikely that we will have a vigorous bounce off of the low.

Like partygoers on a drunken binge, the hangover for this megatop of consumer spending and borrowing will stay with us for a while.

Unemployment rates stayed high well beyond expectations, and even when the numbers dropped, few people believed they accurately reflected the under-employment problems in our economy. Chart 2-J illustrates how pressure in the job market creates ongoing pressure on the housing market. As more people struggle with jobs, mortgage difficulties increase.

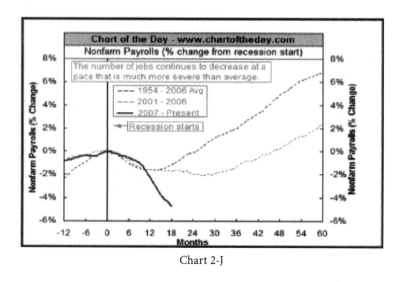

Chart 2-J

MELTDOWN AND THE STOCK MARKET

How will it likely affect stocks and the stock market? In and of itself, a real estate debacle does not necessarily have a devastating effect on the stock market. The 1980s saw a real estate debacle (with a small *d*) during the savings and loan crisis. At one point, 85 percent of the S&Ls in the country were losing money. Most were liquidated or merged out of existence.[9] In fact, the number of banks involved back then was much larger, but the real estate losses were smaller, more contained. Yet the 1980s real estate turmoil barely affected the stock market.

What makes this time different and, indeed, unique is the *magnitude* of losses and the number of people involved, plus the degree of speculation, overvaluation, and leverage. Remembering that this was the bubble to end all bubbles for US real estate should create a lasting image. Nevertheless, if—and I repeat, if—authorities had handled things differently, financial catastrophe might have been averted. So, while it's possible that the next round of foreclosures won't create a huge negative for stocks, it's highly unlikely.

DERIVATIVE NIGHTMARE

However, the real problem was not just real estate, but *the entire financial system*. Leverage was piled on top of leverage. In the next exhibit Chart 2-K shows what famed businessman and investment guru Warren Buffett referred to as "financial weapons of mass destruction," also known as derivatives.

Chart 2-K shows the dollar amount of derivative contracts held by what *were* the five largest US banks at the end of 2007. It shows $172 trillion worth of derivatives versus a total US economy of $14 trillion—more than *ten times the entire US economy* in just the five largest banks! Note: A year after the onset of the real estate crash, the estimate for such contracts was $202 trillion![10]

What are derivatives? To use an analogy—if you had a bunch of grapes and squeezed them, you'd produce either grape juice or wine. Grapes being the underlying product, the wine or the grape juice would be the derivative.

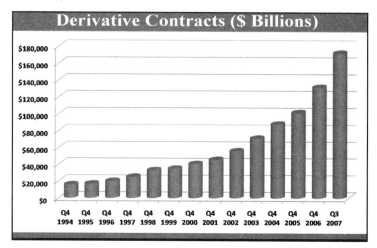

Note: In billions of dollars, national amount of total futures, exchange trader options, over-the-counter options, forwards, and swaps. Data after 1994 does not include spot fix in the total national amount of derivatives.

Chart 2-K

Derivatives are typically entered into by two parties, ostensibly to mitigate or reduce risk. However, risk cannot be eliminated from the entire *system*. For example, certain types of contracts between AIG and our banks were designed to reduce risk. Known as *credit default swaps*, these contracts would pay the banks back in the event that their subprime mortgages defaulted. While this would reduce risks to the individual banks when the subprimes began going bad, from the standpoint of the *system*, the risk was just transferred from one party to another. When large enough amounts of leverage are involved, risk to the *system* remains paramount.

BAILOUTS, BAILOUTS, BAILOUTS

In response to all of this, authorities have resorted to the use of the printing press like never before in history. Next, in Chart 2-L you see the Fed's expansion reserves—a complete vertical climb.

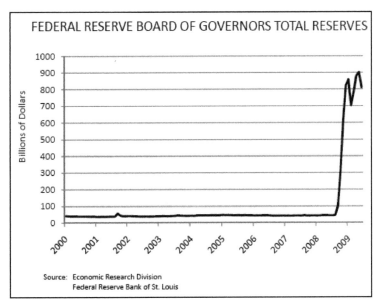

FEDERAL RESERVE BOARD OF GOVERNORS TOTAL RESERVES

Source: Economic Research Division
Federal Reserve Bank of St. Louis

Prepared by Cornerstone Financial Services

Chart 2-L

Prior to the meltdown, the Fed's balance sheet (assets they owned) was under $1 trillion. By the fall of 2014 that total reached $4.5 trillion.[11] This means they bought more than $3 trillion worth of *assets* (call it *bailout*) with money they simply *printed* out of thin air (computer bookkeeping entries).

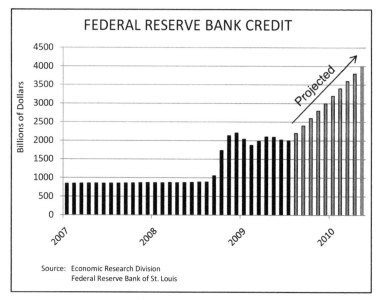

Prepared by Cornerstone Financial Services

Chart 2-M

In the short run these bailouts are *not* inflationary. With banks not lending and consumers not borrowing or spending, the Fed can pump almost unlimited amounts into the system without setting off inflation.

To use a technical term, the *velocity* of money has plummeted (how fast the money turns over within the system). As long as spending and borrowing remain subdued, there will be no inflation problems to deal with. This is depicted in Chart 2-N— the money multiplier, a component of velocity, has plunged. Thus, consumers and businesses are spending less money *and* at a slower pace, which will keep inflation out of the picture for now.

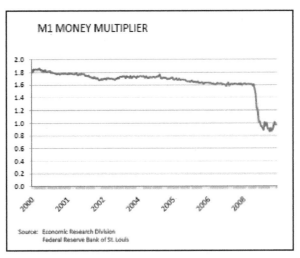

Prepared by Cornerstone Financial Services

Chart 2-N

In the years following the crash of the housing market, deflation remained the primary concern. Inflation is only likely to return much later once the current crisis has passed and Congress has to resort to bailing out Social Security and Medicare. As long as consumers are concerned about their jobs, savings, retirement, and living standard, they will not go back on a spending binge.

Uncertainty, fear, and concerns about the future will predominate for some time, allowing for almost unlimited money printing without causing inflation. However, inflation returns once the velocity of turnover of money in the system increases.

In addition, boomers, the dominant population group, are aging. And aging people become naturally more risk averse as they grow older, especially after seeing their retirement accounts plummet as boomers have.

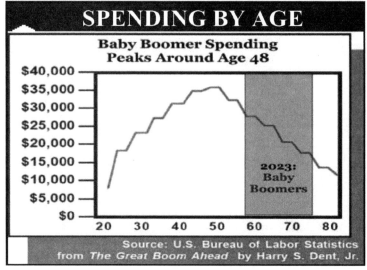

Chart 2-O

In Chart 2-O you see the dilemma. By 2023 boomers will all be well past their peak spending years, which is certain to have a negative influence on the economy.

MORTGAGE MELTDOWN GOES GLOBAL

What started as a US-based housing/mortgage problem soon spilled overseas. Great Britain, much like the United States, also experienced a housing bubble and bust. Ireland hit the wall financially too. Europe, for the most part, appears (believe it or not) in worse condition than we are here in the United States, at least as far as its major banks are concerned.

In 2009 the EU Commission said potentially as much as 44 percent of EU banks' assets were *impaired*. Not only did European banks have their own domestic housing bubbles and busts to deal with, many of them also bought Wall Street's *securitized mortgage assets*. In addition, many loaned money to Eastern European countries that saw their economies crash. These loans of $32.7 billion are mostly denominated in either euros or Swiss francs and will be unrepayable without significant help from international agencies such as the International Monetary Fund (IMF), as the currencies in these countries crashed with their economies.[12]

To deal with the problem, the Bank of England lowered interest rates to its member banks to the lowest levels in 315 years—the entire history of the British Fed.

God, through Ezekiel, has made some very clear and specific revelations in the Bible concerning the rise of a great power to the north of Israel that will destroy the peace and stability of the world at the end of days.

Daniel 9:27 informs us that there will rise on the world's scene a man of supernatural power who, Daniel says, "shall destroy many in their prosperity" (Dan. 8:25, NKJV). This man will come out of the European Union and will try to resolve the Islamic/Israeli dispute now raging in Israel.

This political orator and charismatic personality will make a covenant with Israel for seven years, guaranteeing them safety and protection as a nation. In Scripture he is called the Antichrist, "the son of perdition," meaning Satan's chief son (2 Thess. 2:3, NKJV). When the events of Ezekiel 38 open, the nation of Israel has been given a covenant by this political leader, who is the head of the European Union.

The Jewish people are confident that the European powers will protect them from any outside aggressor or invader. Israel is aware that Russia is its enemy. For years Israel has known that Russia has been helping Iran develop nuclear weapons to be used against them. This seven-year peace accord between the head of the European Union and Israel is in the near future.

—JOHN HAGEE, *Earth's Final Moments*

Further compounding the concerns, by most measures the average European bank is far more highly leveraged than our US-based counterparts. The average European bank is leveraged thirty-eight times the amount of their assets versus twenty-one times for the US banks. *Jiminy Christmas!* These leverage levels are approximately where Bear Stearns and Lehman Brothers were before they failed.

Obviously, we don't know with precision where these bad, highly leveraged loans were hidden, but we certainly knew that there was a lot of smoke—which still exists and indicates a fire. On top of seemingly everyone in the world speculating on risky real estate loans, consumer spending virtually ground to a halt at one point after the market crash and its weakness persists. In late 2014 declining gasoline prices gave consumers some relief, yet even that didn't guarantee we had reached the end of the spending lag.

Look at Chart 2-P, which shows Japanese exports from 2005–2009. The chart says it all.

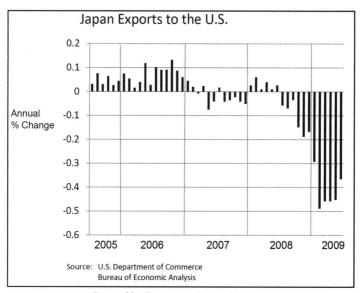

Prepared by Cornerstone Financial Services

Chart 2-P

While emerging Asia seems to be faring better than their more-developed counterparts, obviously they will be negatively affected as this growing global crisis unfolds. Emerging Asian banks largely avoided US and European subprimes, and their banks and debt ratios are much healthier than ours. Asia's problems stem from declining exports, as US and European consumers cut back on spending, a trend destined to last for many years. This will stem from hyper-consumers turning into conservative savers and as more boomers and their European counterparts move into retirement with less to show for their years of hard work than they had anticipated.

In all, the crisis—while it appeared contained in the short term—became the financial equivalent of Chernobyl once the Treasury allowed (or forced) Lehman into bankruptcy. At that moment, deleveraging set in worldwide, and once mass deleveraging sets in, it is very difficult to stop.

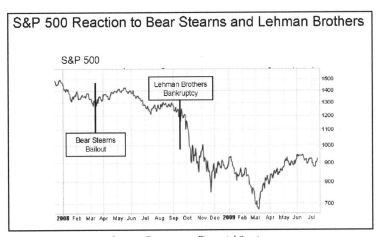

Source: Cornerstone Financial Services

Chart 2-Q

Despite all these problems, central bankers appeared determined to attempt to *inflate* away the problems. But there's no way that $4- or $5-trillion worth of a bailout/stimulus package can offset the estimated $13 trillion of financial and real estate wealth wiped out for American consumers in just one year.

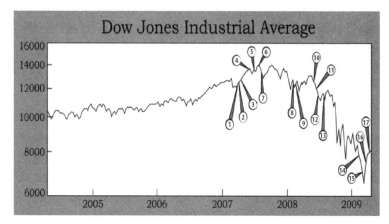

Source: Cornerstone Financial Services

Chart 2-R

Each of the numbers on Chart 2-R link to the correlated number in the following list. Take a look at the responses of authorities as this long-term crisis was unfolding.

1. "The fallout in subprime mortgages is going to be painful to some lenders, but it is largely contained."
—Treasury Secretary Henry Paulson on March 13, 2007[13]

2. "At this juncture...the impact on the broader economy and financial markets of the problems in the subprime markets seems likely to be contained."
—Federal Reserve Chairman Ben Bernanke on March 28, 2007[14]

3. "I don't see (subprime mortgage market troubles) imposing a serious problem. I think it's going to be

largely contained.... All the signs I look at [show]
the housing market is at or near the bottom."
—Treasury Secretary Henry Paulson
on April 20, 2007[15]

4. "Given the fundamental factors in place that should
support the demand for housing, we believe the
effect of the troubles in the subprime sector on the
broader housing market will likely be limited."
—Federal Reserve Chairman Ben Bernanke
on May 17, 2007[16]

5. "This is far and away the strongest global economy
I've seen in my business lifetime."
—Treasury Secretary Henry Paulson
on July 12, 2007[17]

6. "I don't think it [the subprime mess] poses any
threat to the overall economy."
—Treasury Secretary Henry Paulson
on July 26, 2007[18]

7. "I see the underlying economy as being very healthy."
—Treasury Secretary Henry Paulson
on August 1, 2007[19]

8. "[The US economy] is fundamentally strong,
diverse and resilient."
—Treasury Secretary Henry Paulson
on February 14, 2008[20]

9. "I expect there will be some failures.... I don't
anticipate any serious problems of that sort [capital
ratios] among the large internationally active banks
that make up a very substantial part of our banking
system."
—Federal Reserve Chairman Ben Bernanke
on February 28, 2008[21]

10. "The worst is likely to be behind us."
> —Treasury Secretary Henry Paulson
> on May 7, 2008[22]

11. "In my judgment, we are closer to the end of the market turmoil than the beginning."
> —Treasury Secretary Henry Paulson
> on May 16, 2008[23]

12. "The risk that the economy has entered a substantial downturn appears to have diminished over the past month or so."
> —Federal Reserve Chairman Ben Bernanke
> on June 9, 2008[24]

13. "Our banking system is a safe and a sound one... this is a very manageable situation... our regulators are focused on it."
> —Treasury Secretary Henry Paulson
> on July 20, 2008[25]

14. "We will have to try things we've never tried before. We will make mistakes. We will go through periods in which things get worse and progress is uneven or interrupted."
> —Treasury Secretary Timothy Geithner
> on February 10, 2009[26]

15. "We've put in place a comprehensive strategy designed to attack this crisis on all fronts. It's a strategy to create jobs, to help responsible homeowners, to restart lending, and to grow our economy over the long term. And we are beginning to see signs of progress."
> —President Barack Obama
> on March 24, 2009[27]

16. "The sense of a ball falling off a table, which is what the economy has felt like since the middle of last fall, I think we can be reasonably confident that that is going to end within the next few months, and we will no longer have that sense of free-fall."
—National Economic Council
Director Larry Summers
on April 9, 2009[28]

17. "Recently we have seen tentative signs that the sharp decline in economic activity may be slowing."
—Federal Reserve Chairman Ben Bernanke
on April 14, 2009[29]

My final thought on these matters? Years after these reassuring statements from top national leaders, it still looks to me as if the great financial storm of the twenty-first century is far from over. We are bracing for the big chill yet to come.

CHAPTER 3

WEATHERING THE FINANCIAL STORM

By Jerry Tuma

H AVE YOU DEVELOPED a strategy to help your family cope with the economic crisis our world is facing today? In this chapter you will learn to understand the root causes of many of your financial difficulties and develop some wise solutions to help you and your loved ones weather the financial storm that erupted in 2008. You will be able to apply these principles to our current economic crisis, but they will be useful for your future and even your children's futures. An economy—whether individual, family, community, national, or world—runs in cycles. What you are learning you can apply to situations you face in the future as well.

As a veteran of the industry with more than thirty years as a Certified Financial Planner professional, I certainly believe that personal financial planning is important.

SEVEN STEPS TO FINANCIAL FREEDOM

Let me give you some simple steps that you can take to assess your current financial situation and determine how to protect

your family against financial crisis.[1] These are basic fundamentals
that should apply to most families.

1. *Take inventory*: If you have ever gotten lost while
   driving in a strange city, you now know the importance of finding out where you are in order to
   figure out how to get where you want to go. That is
   the first step to achieving financial freedom.

2. *Buy adequate life insurance*: A good rule of thumb
   for a young family with children at home is to buy
   life insurance on the breadwinner equal to ten
   times that person's earnings. This will give you a
   lump sum of money that can be invested to replace
   that income.

3. *Pay off all consumer debts*: This includes credit
   cards and finance companies—anything beyond
   your automobile and home. These consumer debts
   are the worst form of debt since they primarily represent consumption and not investment, and carry
   the highest rates of interest. First cut all unnecessary spending, and apply that freed-up money
   toward your smallest debt first. Each time you pay
   off a debt, take the monthly payment you had been
   making and use those additional funds exclusively
   for further reduction on your next-highest debt. It
   may take you several years to get out of debt, but
   this is the best way to do it.

4. *Start an emergency reserve*: We advise that you set
   aside two to three months' living expenses—the
   bare-bones amount on which you could live—in
   an emergency reserve fund. This could be a bank
   account, an interest-bearing money market fund,
   or something similar. Ideally, we recommend that

people build up at least three to six months' income in conservative, liquid accounts.

5. *Begin a long-term savings plan*: Little by little, accumulate assets.

6. *Pay off your automobiles*: Financially, your best bet is to buy a reliable automobile and drive it as long as possible. Buy used cars, service them, and keep them running. The second alternative is to buy an inexpensive new car, service it well (changing the oil regularly), and keep it for a *long* time.

7. *Prepay on your home*: Prepaying on a home can save thousands and even hundreds of thousands of dollars, regardless of whether you have a fixed or variable rate mortgage.

Look closely at each of these steps to find creative ways to adapt for this latest crisis, as they are arranged in order of priority. The first priority for achieving financial security is cutting back on spending to eliminate consumer debt. Take these ideas and strategize specific solutions to get rid of debt. Remember that *change creates opportunities, and challenging times create the best opportunities!*

Often the best way to learn is to study the example of someone who has already done this. There are people who are living debt free and prospering right now—right in the midst of a world gone financially amok. Look at the lives of some of these individuals, and let their sound financial wisdom influence your practices and strategies.

A book that I strongly recommend is *The Millionaire Next Door*, written by Thomas Stanley and William Danko.[2] It is one of the most comprehensive studies on wealth ever done in the history in America. It isn't a flashy, get-rich-quick manual. It involves the slow process of becoming successful in your career or business, saving up your money instead of spending it, budgeting down to the last cent, investing carefully and prodigiously, seeking out good advice when necessary, and spending a tremendous amount of time on money matters.[3] Covering more than twenty years of study by two academic teams, this group set out to study millionaires and their habits and, furthermore, what made them millionaires to begin with. Of the five hundred millionaires interviewed, only 19 percent had received any income or wealth from a trust fund or estate, and fewer than 20 percent inherited more than 10 percent of their wealth. Take a look at some of the interesting factors this book uncovered about millionaires.

SEVEN FACTORS ABOUT MILLIONAIRES

The image of most millionaires as children of privilege born with the proverbial silver spoon in their mouth doesn't square with research that shows:

1. They live well below their means.

2. They allocate their time, energy, and money efficiently, in ways conducive to building wealth.

3. They believe that financial independence is more important than displaying high social status.

4. Their parents did not provide economic outpatient care.

5. Their adult children are economically self-sufficient.

6. They are proficient in targeting market opportunities.

7. They chose the right occupation.[4]

What do most millionaires say they learned? "Think differently from the crowd."[5] One of the most important principles we can learn from this book is that most millionaires are frugal in how they spend their money. They believe in little or no personal debt. When they do go into debt, it is usually with the purpose of going into business, buying a house or property, or acquiring an education. They never spend money frivolously.

Because these people typically were out of debt (most of them owned their own businesses, though not all), when there was a downturn in the economy or in their market, they weathered the storm and came out on the other side with a larger market share. In this case, difficult or challenging times surely proved to be an opportunity—a longer-term blessing!

This is the mentality you should have going into the coming demographic winter. Don't look at this negatively, as a half-empty glass. Look at this as an opportunity. Certainly, in our view there could be great devastation occurring to the wealth and the livelihoods of many people in the United States, primarily among those planning as if everything will continue without change and are not prepared. Those who lead high-consumptive lifestyles and those who are overleveraged (with large debts) will be the first to suffer.

PROTECT YOUR CAPITAL

First, do your best to grow or at least protect your capital. Be aware of what is going on in the market and be ready if there is a point in time to get out of the market. Keep in mind that if we are in a secular (long-term) bear market, as I believe we are, there will likely be shorter-term, cyclical bounces along the way that could be spectacular. To know what to do, you must stay current and be ready for the next phase of this crisis. Learn alternative strategies for managing your assets, or hire someone who can assist you. For the near term, you may want to focus on preserving capital or possibly use *inverse strategies*, which I will explain shortly. The simplest approach to take in a deflationary environment is high-quality, fixed-income, and absolute-return strategies. Yes, the stock market has increased in recent years, but keep in mind that it is likely to continue having huge bounces from time to time.

If you feel, as I do, that our current economic situation is a potential Category 5 hurricane, you may not want to stay in the market on a buy-and-hold basis (a long-term investment strategy based on the view that in the long run, financial markets give a good rate of return despite periods of volatility or decline.)[6] Why? Because, in my opinion, there are periods of time in history when buy-and-hold has failed miserably—such as in the 1930s and the 1970s.

At the conclusion of Ezekiel 37, the nation of Israel had been physically reborn. Today they have a flag; they have a constitution; they have a prime minister and a Knesset. They have a police force, a powerful military might, and the world's best intelligence agencies. They have Jerusalem, the City of God. They have a nation.

They have everything but spiritual life. Like the dry bones of Ezekiel 37, Israel awaits the spiritual awakening of the breath of God and the coming of Messiah.

—JOHN HAGEE, *Earth's Final Moments*

I'm not necessarily advising you to get out of the market, as I have no way of knowing when you'll read this book or exactly what will be happening in the economy or market at that time. I can't give blanket recommendations, anyway. For a better understanding of the current environment, check out our radio show and our Web site at www.cornerstonereport.com.

Inverse strategies, or *absolute-return strategies*, aim to produce a positive absolute return regardless of the direction of financial markets.[7] These return strategies are typically not something that people can easily learn on their own. If you have a 401(k), you likely do not even have access to these types of accounts. A more astute investor will know how to use an absolute-return strategy that has the potential to make money when the market is going down. Inverse strategies are difficult to pull off; unless you are an experienced, astute investor, you should not try this on your own. If you do not know what an inverse strategy is—or understand how to use it—that is a good indication you probably should not attempt this strategy on your own. Hire someone to assist you.

I believe we have entered a secular bear phase that could last a long time. We don't know exactly what is coming or when, but the demographics and the number of people that have passed their peak spending period do not indicate another boom phase like this until at least 2023. That is a long time!

In my opinion, before we have another lasting stock market boom, the demographics are going to have to turn around—and that is a long way off. I like to apply the principle from the legendary best-seller *Good to Great*, which says, "You must never confuse faith that you will prevail in the end—which you can never afford to lose—with the discipline to confront the most brutal facts of your current reality, whatever they might be."[8]

That is why I am devoting a chapter to "financial triage," or developing wise solutions to weather this financial storm. You need to first stop the bleeding. There may be a time when you want to get on the sidelines and see if this develops into a worse storm and, if it does, be ready with the solutions that are going to protect your financial future.

DETERMINE YOUR EXIT STRATEGY

There is an old philosophy we use at my investment firm (many other investors follow this same guideline): "Buy low and sell high." If the current storm becomes more pronounced—as I think it will—it might be more accurately stated, "Attempt to sell high, and then later buy low."

Way back in early 2000, our firm warned people to get out

of stocks entirely. Since that time, the regulations governing this industry have changed. Now I could not tell a person to get completely out of the stock market even if I wanted to. However, when we were telling everyone to get out in 2000, nearly everyone else was telling them to get rich quick with tech stocks or dot-coms. Close to 80 percent of the money flowing into the market the first quarter of 2000 went into technology stocks. Meanwhile, we advised our clients and radio listeners to get out, which made us contrarians. If you got out anywhere near the top of the NASDAQ, almost three years later, by October of 2002 many of the dot-com survivors—the companies that supposedly were going to make it after the bubble crashed—*had a total market value that was less than their cash in the bank.* That was certainly a "buy low" opportunity at that point.[9]

The issue is: I don't believe that most people will enjoy attempting to ride this storm out on a buy-and-hold basis. Most people have been in denial; not wanting to go through the pain of loss, they delay a decision. But we must face the future.

SUPPLY AND DEMAND

I am reminded of the bumper sticker that says, "I am spending my children's inheritance," seen frequently in places such as sunny Florida. With the demographic storm of recent years taking huge chunks of capital out of the securities markets and most Americans' finances, is there any likelihood that boomers— as they reach retirement age in mammoth proportions—might decide to use some of those assets for retirement income or for a more comfortable standard of living?

Several years ago during a coaching session with a group of financial planners in San Diego, I commented, "You work with clients every day; you do financial plans and work to help people accumulate financial assets. What do you think is the likelihood that the vast majority of those people would like to *spend* some of those assets in their retirement years?"

The answer was unanimous—*yes*, most of them will want to spend some of their assets. The vast majority of Americans will spend all or part of their financial assets as they retire. Given the upcoming environment, it's also possible that many may decide not to retire. The vast majority of people are not content to simply live on pensions and Social Security while passing on the vast majority of their assets to their heirs.

However, what happens to the supply-and-demand balance for stocks, bonds, and other financial assets when more boomers start spending their assets? This is not to say that there won't be investments that will go up in this kind of environment. In fact, the objective of our firm is to find assets that will prosper during tough times. Yet, those who continue to expect the same performance of the recent past in the near future are likely stepping into a gigantic hole. As investment expert Jeremy Siegel commented in his book *The Future for Investors*: "Assets such as stocks and bonds have no intrinsic value—you cannot eat your stock certificates. The only way their value can be realized is by selling them, and you can sell them only if there are enough willing buyers."[10]

Siegel's comment is especially relevant when considering those who reach the point of being ready to cash in their assets. Assets can be turned into purchasing power *only if someone else is willing to give up his or her consumption so you can enjoy yours.*

Throughout history when the younger generation reached middle age, they have had sufficient purchasing power to buy their parents' assets. But this time it is different. There are not nearly enough Generation Xers (the generation born in the late 1960s and 1970s) with sufficient wealth to absorb the boomers' substantial portfolio of stocks and bonds.

The looming problem of the boomer population is reminiscent of an old Wall Street story. A broker recommends that his client buy a small speculative stock with good earnings prospects. The investor purchases the stock, accumulating thousands of shares at ever-rising prices. Patting himself on the back, he phones his broker, instructing him to sell all his shares. His broker snaps back, "Sell? Sell to whom? You're the only one who has been buying the stock!"

The words "Sell? Sell to whom?" might haunt baby boomers over the next decade. Who are the buyers of the trillions of dollars of boomer assets? The generation that swept politics, fashion, and the media in the last half of the twentieth century produced an *age wave* that threatens to drown in their financial assets. The consequences could be disastrous not only for the boomers' retirement but also for the economic health of the entire population.[11]

It is *not* positive for the market that most of these people will begin to spend some of their assets at some point in time. Why is that? Who, pray tell, is going to buy these assets? Remember, all markets work on supply and demand. How does a generation seventy-six million strong sell portions of their stocks and bonds to a generation *with only forty-one million people* (baby busters)? How can boomers sell their trophy homes to a generation just over half their size? As they spend (or sell) their financial assets, someone has to buy them. For every sale there has to be a buyer on the opposite end purchasing those assets.

The supply-and-demand numbers simply don't wash. That is, unless you somehow *hope* that foreigners, people who are not citizens of America, will continue to buy enough of America to bail out the boomers. Having most of America owned by non-American citizens is obviously not a good solution, either.

For more than three thousand years the Jews celebrated the exodus of Moses from Egypt's bondage as the greatest event in their history. Yet Jeremiah 16:14–15 (NKJV) declares there is coming a second exodus that will be so great that the first exodus will pale by comparison.

Jeremiah states that the people will come from "the land of the north," which I believe is Russia. In the Bible, all directions are given from Jerusalem. In the mind of God, Jerusalem is the center of the universe.

Jeremiah expanded his prophecy of Exodus II to include "all the lands where He had driven them." Although Exodus II is far from complete, as the mighty right hand of God continues to gather "the apple of His eye" to the land given to Abraham and his seed almost six thousand years ago.

—JOHN HAGEE, *Earth's Final Moments*

There has been and likely will continue to be a future boom in Asia that will play into the economics. But let me ask you this: If you were a foreign investor and could put your money anywhere in the world that you wanted, would you pick an American economy with a rapidly aging population, or would you pick the highest-performing growth areas of the world? Where would you put your money? Would you put it into an aging society with enormous entitlement (Social Security, Medicare) problems, or would you put it into areas of the world where growth is the most exciting? Hasn't China complained about our long-term financial picture and discussed alternatives to the US dollar with other countries?[12]

We can learn from the experience of Japan's market when their society began to age after their demographics topped out in 1989. No foreigners (including the United States) rushed in to take the Japanese's financial assets. No one wanted to catch a falling knife; no one knew where the bottom of the Japanese market would end. Few investors were attracted to Japan once their bubble popped. There was no long-term solution—just a long time of pain before the Japanese market finally bottomed out.

There will be new products, new services, new companies, and new growth occurring in America as our businesses continue to innovate as well as fragment into smaller and smaller units. There will be opportunities, and there will be places to make money—without question. But, looking at the US economy, stock market, and financial assets as a whole, are they likely to be the most attractive to pull in mass numbers of buyers from foreign sources? Or are they more likely to be putting their money into more dynamic growth areas of the world? The answer is fairly obvious. Most of these investors would prefer to put their money into the more dramatic growth areas.

The issue we face with the boomer age wave is not negativity, *but reality*. In order to weather this financial storm, we must learn how to play the game in a way that wins instead of loses. Seek to develop wise solutions that will allow you to face your financial problems head-on, not wavering or hiding or sticking your head in the sand. The ostrich approach leaves you quite vulnerable to a swift kick in the pants.

WISE SOLUTIONS FOR SMALL BUSINESS

In economic downtimes individual consumers cut back to the bare necessities in their personal and family finances. As a small-business owner or large-corporate CEO, you will want to be in a business that will be somewhat resistant to recessionary (or worse) times. Consider whether or not your product, industry, or field is something that people can't live without and whether or not it fits an aging population or challenging times. As we head into the chill of this demographic winter, if you are a business owner, you will want to assess the value of your business to people in an economic downturn and develop solutions that will help you to weather the storm.

Some businesses will be resistant to the downturn; others will not. Ask yourself, "Am I trying to ride a dead horse, and do I need to change fields in order to adjust? Or should I persevere *through* the challenging times in order to gain more market share?" The answer will be different for each individual and business or industry. Just keep in mind, it is likely to be *nearly a decade* before the next boom. That's a long time. Some technologies, service fields, and products could be completely different or obsolete within ten years.

You should go into the economic downturn looking forward to weathering whatever storm comes. Anticipate increasing your market share. Consider this upcoming time as a time of *great wealth transfer*. As I mentioned earlier, the Great Depression of the 1930s was the worst economic period our country has ever seen. Indeed, it was the worst in the modern history of the world.

The lesson learned from that chapter of our history is that it is possible to make enormous amounts of money during difficult times. More millionaires were created per capita during the Great Depression than in any other time in US history. This same kind of great wealth transfer will almost certainly take place in this financial storm, going from the hands of the unprepared to the hands of the prepared. Remember the football adage: "Luck is what happens when preparation meets opportunity." I encourage you to get prepared, because the opportunity is just about to knock on your door.

PROSPERING IN A HOSTILE ECONOMY

Some of the better opportunities America—and each person in America—will likely see in the longer-term future will come as we face increasing shortages of raw materials and energy sources. While in the short run, deflationary forces during future years will doubtless keep commodity prices low, over the new few decades prices could explode. Similar to the shortages of the 1970s brought on by the baby boomer generation, the world—including America—will need to create new opportunities and sources for these assets as countries such as China and India continue growing toward first-world status over the next decade or two.

The world is not suffering from permanent deprivation or scarce or limited resources. But there have been explosive demands for new raw materials and energy as the result of nearly one-third of mankind moving toward free enterprise. Deprivation caused by Mao's communist system and India's socialism finally yielded to forward-thinking officials who moved their countries and respective populations into the twenty-first century, poised to become economic leaders within a few decades.

As the next two decades unfold, there is a much greater likelihood that natural resources (especially oil) will become increasingly scarce, given current economic growth rates in China and India as they move from bicycles and public transportation to individually owned autos.

With a collective population of more than 2.5 billion and growing, and booming economic growth, China and India are going to play an increasingly important role in global economic matters and energy markets.[13]

For many decades no other country was to compete with the United States's huge domestic auto market, where sixteen to seventeen million vehicles were sold each year. That is now changing. Even as the economic crash of 2008 sent America's auto industry reeling, the emerging markets of China and India became large enough to support world-scale domestic manufacturing. India is still on a relatively small scale, but in recent years China's market reached half the size of the United States and continues to grow.[14]

While the current ownership ratio of cars in China is low as a percentage of their population, officials have invested in mass highway infrastructure in anticipation of many more drivers. China's population and industrial output are mainly concentrated within the economically higher developed east coast, meaning that raw materials—especially coal—have to be transported from the far northwestern and northeastern provinces via railways or inland waterways. The government hasn't paid much attention to road conditions and access in many rural areas. However, China's national roads reached a total of 192 million kilometers in 2005, with $240 billion spent in the first half of that decade.[15]

The automotive industry in India is one of their largest industries and a key sector of the economy. India's Tata Motors production of the Nano, which debuted in 2008 around $2,000 before its price rose, placed auto ownership directly within the grasp of many Chinese and Indians based upon their incomes (and was expected to arrive in the US in 2015).[16] The old saying "You ain't seen nothing yet" likely holds true for India, China, and the rest of emerging Asia for the foreseeable future, as the bulk of the world's economic growth is likely to come from this region for at least the next decade. The United States and especially Europe are aging cultures. This creates great potential for profit for those who catch this mammoth wave, which could make the baby boomer wave look small in comparison before it's over.

Ultimately, if only a portion of the 2.5 billion-plus people in India and China move into some semblance of middle-class income within their respective countries, it will produce enormous growth. Since much of this growth revolves around creating and developing infrastructure, raw materials, and energy, plus technology, will likely see the greatest gains.

ENERGY

Below you see a table showing the percentage of the world's energy that still comes from fossil fuels. Note that 10 percent comes from nonnuclear renewable sources.

2006 Energy Supply[17]	
Fossil	79 percent
Nuclear	11 percent
Renewable	10 percent

While I'm absolutely in favor of developing solar, wind, and other renewable resources, the fact remains that all renewable energy sources currently provide 10 percent of the world's energy supply, and those sources cannot possibly grow fast enough to keep up with burgeoning demand in Asia. You simply can't get there from here.

As China and India industrialize and move deeper into the

twenty-first century, incredible demands will be placed upon raw materials and energy. Therefore, the best policy would be not only to encourage renewable sources of energy but also to radically accelerate the discovery of fossil fuels as well.

At the end of the day we will need all of the above in large quantities to support emerging Asia and the rest of the world. Holding an ideologically pure stance on ecology simply won't work and will likely produce more pain (again) in terms of very high costs for gasoline and potential fuel shortages.

You can worry all you want about global warming, but I can guarantee you that more than 2.5 billion Indians and Chinese care more about driving cars than melting icebergs. Given the future possibilities, right now is the best time to encourage energy development, not waiting until the next crisis. An "all of the above" energy policy is what we need.

Oil Rig Count[18]		
	Year	**Count**
Peak	1981	6,200
Bottom	1999	1,200
	2004	2,500

As you can see, the number of active drilling rigs worldwide peaked at 6,200 in 1981 and bottomed at only 1,200 in 1999. Given the long lead times necessary to bring oil products online (as long as five years or more), it was no coincidence we experienced a mini energy shock in 2007 and early 2008. The energy supply got behind the curve compared to the great increases in global demand.

With Asia's energy needs starting to skyrocket and production growing only slowly, it was only a matter of time until demand caught up with supply. While the global recession reduced demand, nothing has been done to fix the longer-term problem. Longer term, expect more problems with energy shortages unless a radical change occurs in current US energy policy.

In the following graph, the Energy Information Administration

(EIA) estimated that with the average world growth in GDP at 3.8 percent, the world's energy needs will increase nearly 50 percent from 2003 until 2030. Given burgeoning demand for energy in China and India, these projections look way too conservative to me.

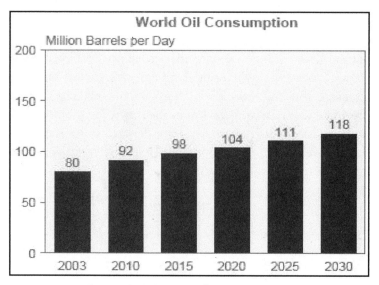

Source: U.S. Energy Information Agency

Chart 3-A

LOOK PAST THE VALLEY

While no one can be certain about the economic future, my belief is that we are going to have an extreme period of challenging times during the next decade. However, longer term, I see the potential for great optimism.

As hordes of people come out of formerly repressed societies such as China and India and as undeveloped countries become developed countries, the world's potential for long-term prosperity is truly staggering.

I personally believe that America, as a nation, has a calling.

Our Founding Fathers believed that the purpose of America was truly to be "a city on a hill," as articulated by John Winthrop as he pulled into Boston harbor in 1630: "For we must consider that we shall be as a city upon a hill. The eyes of all people are upon us."[19] Somewhat like God's original plan for Israel of old, as the pilgrims came to the United States, they received inspiration they believed to be from God, stating that this country was essentially going to show the rest of the world how to do it. And in many ways, we have. With just over 5 percent of the world's population, we produce approximately one-third of all the goods and services in the world. In terms of military might, the next twenty most populated countries *combined* do not add up to the military might of the United States. While certainly this does not make us immune to terrorist attacks or impervious to all challenges, it does demonstrate that many, many of the things that our Founding Fathers set up in our society proved to be the best solutions yet created for man.

The problem is that we have gotten off the path and deviated from their ideals. While we certainly don't want to let our freedom become moral license, it is important for us to remember that there is a strong and definite correlation between freedom and prosperity. The freer a society, the more economically prosperous it will tend to be.

While we all have certain rights, we must also all yield those rights in certain instances for the betterment and common good of the country. Sometimes we must sacrifice our own personal freedoms for the betterment of society as a whole. This is one of the things that America has historically been good at. There is a moral underpinning to our society that was originally based, in part, upon the Ten Commandments of God and the Christian heritage of our forefathers.

As I look toward the future and look *past* the valley, I see the opportunity for incredible things happening to seven billion people around the world if they emulate our best qualities and not our worst.

Truly, in terms of economic activity, foundational principles, freedoms, rule of law, property rights, and all the things that have made America great, America is a worthy example for other countries to emulate. I believe this can lead to an even greater level of overall prosperity, freedom, and enjoyment for the rest of the world. I consider America an *evangelist* to the rest of the world in terms of many of the right principles for financial prosperity. It has been America's destiny to shine as a "city on a hill," to model the way to "life, liberty, and the pursuit of happiness." It can continue to be if we will answer *the call*.

CHAPTER 4

GROWING YOUR WAY TO PROSPERITY

By Jerry Tuma

I N THE FIRST chapter I looked at the economic problems brought on by limiting our population growth. In addition to this area, we should also look for business solutions that will continue to make America great. Above all, we must understand this *does not* involve the movement toward excess regulation and taxation. Most politicians, when pushed into a corner, will demand excess regulation in order to attempt to stop "abuses." Then they demand higher rates of taxation to pay for the social programs they want to adopt. For most of them, that's how they got elected—by promising the electorate the most goodies from the government.

No matter how much we may not like the fact, the government is limited in how much it can accomplish. Yet, the government *can* be a very effective force for good. Think of the government as a lever. You can use a crowbar to move a two-ton boulder if you use it correctly, at the right place and time. Government can provide extremely good leverage in either a positive or negative sense.

If you look at the history of tax policy and regulation, you will find that any time the government goes into a period of excessive—even obsessive—focus on regulation, the economy generally stagnates (like in the 1970s). After the financial scandals and debacles of the past two decades, our government began implementing more regulation and shifting the direction of the Reagan revolution.

Excessive regulation, as well as a well-meaning desire to keep the *crooks and idiots* from ripping-off the public, in the long run usually ends up hurting honest people far more than the crooks. Overall, the damage to the system is often much higher due to zealous overregulation. Such steps simply add massive bureaucracies with which the average business and consumer must deal.

Think of it as a race. For the United States to stay competitive economically, it must do everything it can to make our *Olympic business runners* the fastest in the world. Encourage our runners with good nutrition, training, the best facilities, and the best equipment. Do everything that we can do to make them the best.

This would not involve carrying another person. Have you ever seen an Olympic runner win a race while carrying another person strapped to his or her back? Excessive regulation and taxation is the equivalent of trying to win the Olympic 400-meter relay with our anchor runner carrying another person.

In 2015 government of all forms made up approximately 21 percent of our country's annual production (gross domestic product)[1], and since has followed an upward trend. Waste that is created because of excess regulation creates an environment in which it becomes increasingly difficult to do business and continue competing with the best in the global marketplace.

The same is true of excessive taxation. During the coming demographic winter, the most likely thing that will happen is politicians deciding: "We need more tax revenue to pay for these social programs, and the answer is to raise tax rates." In the long run this is *not* the right answer. Raising tax rates *suppresses* economic activity, thus leaving a smaller economic pie from which to generate taxes.

In fact, studies by Harvard University PhD Robert Barro and by highly regarded Italian economist Roberto Perotti both concluded independently of each other that every dollar spent by the federal government reduces private spending (consumer or corporate) by one dollar, with no net improvement to the GDP. Government spending will, however, increase the national debt, thus increasing the national debt without a net improvement in the economy.[2] The answer should be *increasing the size of the pie.* By *lowering* tax rates and reducing excess regulation, you create *free enterprise zones* that will be more conducive to world-class business practices. Thus, you attract more businesses, as well as businessmen and women from all over the world. Creating an environment that is difficult to work in, for a particular locale, will tend to encourage people to move elsewhere. We have seen this happen in many states within the United States.

There are obvious exceptions to this, but generally speaking, intrastate migration is occurring. In general the migration is moving *away* from more highly regulated, higher cost-of-living states toward lower cost-of-living, lower-regulation states. Remember, more population translates into increased economic growth and prosperity.

TOP TEN OUTBOUND AND INBOUND STATES, 2003–2007[3]

Top Ten OUTBOUND States		Top Ten INBOUND States	
State	**Five-Year Average**	**State**	**Five-Year Average**
North Dakota	66.4 percent	North Carolina	62.0 percent
Michigan	63.3 percent	Nevada	61.7 percent
New Jersey	60.9 percent	Oregon	61.0 percent
Indiana	60.0 percent	South Carolina	59.8 percent
New York	59.5 percent	Idaho	59.3 percent
Illinois	58.5 percent	Alabama	58.3 percent
Pennsylvania	56.3 percent	Arizona	58.3 percent
Ohio	55.2 percent	Tennessee	55.3 percent

Top Ten OUTBOUND States		Top Ten INBOUND States	
State	Five-Year Average	State	Five-Year Average
Wisconsin	54.6 percent	Delaware	55.2 percent
Massachusetts	54.5 percent	New Mexico	54.6 percent

With the exception of North Dakota—which even after the fracking boom of recent years, still has fewer than 1 million residents and a harsh climate—the other outbound states are generally high-tax/regulation "blue" states. There are seven states that do not impose an income tax on individuals: Alaska, Florida, Nebraska, North Dakota, Texas, Washington, and Wyoming. Two additional states tax only dividend and interest income: New Hampshire and Tennessee. Looking at it purely from a tax perspective, between 1995 and 2007, the ten highest tax states lost 1.7 million people, while the ten lowest tax states gained 1.3 million. Population movement within the United States is also moving away from states with the highest tax burdens toward states with lower tax burdens. Migration means more people—hence, greater economic activity.

States such as New Jersey and California, because of excessive government policies, tax rates, and regulation, have pushed the cost of living and of doing business too high. Thus, many businesses have moved to different parts of the country so that they can better grow their companies. US firms compete with foreign corporations, and if the latter can do it better and cheaper, they will take away our market share. In order to compete, many companies have been forced to relocate to other parts of the country that are friendlier to businesses, with fewer regulations, lower tax structures, and lower utility costs.

One example is Buck Knives. One of the world's leading manufacturers of hunting and fishing knives since 1902, this third-generation, family-owned business is legendary among hunters and outdoorsmen. Yet, due to rising costs (regulations, taxes, utilities, labor, etc.), Buck Knives found itself unable to stay ahead of its leading competitor and began steadily losing market share. After a long and exhaustive research, the CEO of Buck Knives, A. J. Buck, made the decision to move Buck's corporate headquarters from San Diego, California, to Post Falls, Idaho, in late 2004 and reduced its costs by an estimated 30 percent. After virtually every category of expense that Buck faced had been reduced drastically, the company experienced an upswing.[4]

This will likely be an ongoing story over the next two decades as corporations move their headquarters to more favorable business climates. Hopefully, politicians will not respond to upcoming pressures by imposing major tax increases, which will suppress economic activity. While I am not holding my breath on this, the odds are high that those states that legislatively favor growing businesses and fostering business-friendly climates will continue to attract corporate ventures and new business.

Ezekiel puts extreme emphasis on the fact that Israel's great enemy would come from the "uttermost north." It is mentioned in Ezekiel 38:6 and 15, and again in Ezekiel 39:2. The King James Version doesn't translate this as accurately as do the Revised Standard Version and the Amplified Bible. The Hebrew word that qualifies north means either "uttermost" or "extreme north." Any map will instantly verify that the extreme north from Israel is Russia.

—JOHN HAGEE, *Earth's Final Moments*

A good example of unintentional consequences was a luxury tax passed in January 1991. Democratic leaders decided that they wanted to increase taxes on the *rich* in order to create a *fairer* sharing of the economic pie (and as attempt to raise government revenue), so they imposed a luxury tax on yachts and other expensive items.

Did the rich get hurt? No, the rich decided to stop buying yachts.

(People change behavior based upon incentives.) The people who got hurt were the yacht manufacturers and workers who lost their jobs when their companies went broke. This bill bankrupted several manufacturers and cost the jobs of the *average guys*—the people Democrats were trying to help in the first place. Not only that, but the business failures and lost wages actually created less tax revenue, the exact opposite of what was intended.[5] We call this *the law of unintended consequences*, and politicians are masters at it.

Our objective should not be to create more hurdles and difficulties for American businesses, but rather to free up the capitalist system to attract as much capital, labor, manpower, and brainpower to the United States as possible.

As has been the case in the past, we should make the United States the *best* free-enterprise zone in the world. We should make it a *very* attractive place to do business, more than ever before. If we do this, we will not be able to keep the people, manpower, knowledge, and capital *out* of the United States. Going backward into a policy of progressive taxation and regulation will be choosing the wrong direction. We would effectively be placing a person on the back of our sprinters. Please, Mr. Politician, don't do this.

SMALL BUSINESS SOLUTION

What other solutions are possible to fix the consumer spending problems? As I mentioned earlier, people tend to hit peak spending when they have teenagers in their families. During the demographic winter (approximately between the years 2009 and 2023), if consumer spending becomes as big of a problem as we expect it will, this in turn will trigger a domino effect. First, it will affect the profitability of American corporations, which then affects their corporate earnings, the price of the company stock, and their 401(k) plans. This, in turn, affects both the ability of average Americans to retire, plus the value of their retirement accounts. Not a good situation. A chain reaction occurs, as one level of spending and problems spills over into another and another—and the string of dominos falls.

But is it possible to fix the consumer-spending problem? Again, the answer is *yes*, long term, but is not going to be obvious to most politicians. By training, most are lawyers with little or no economic training or background. Consumer-spending problems can only be solved by encouraging patriotic immigration— encouraging more and more businesses to come to the United States to set up shop—and *not* by discouraging businesses through excessive taxation and regulation, thus pushing more businesses off shore. We should encourage the proliferation of small business.

GREAT TRANSFORMATIONS

In recent years America, as well as the rest of the world, has been going through a series of great transformations on four fronts. These four transformations were discussed in an excellent speech in 2009 by *Herbert Meyer*, a special assistant to the director of the Central Intelligence Agency during the Reagan administration— and recipient of the Congressional Medal of Honor for being the first person to recognize and predict that the Soviet Union was about to collapse.

One of the transformations Meyer discussed was the "shifting demographics of Western civilization," caused because "most countries in the Western world have stopped breeding." Another transformation is the "restructuring of American business," as former developing countries become first-world, twenty-first-century, Internet-age countries.[6]

In Meyer's example, the fracturing of American business is positive, not negative. It means that larger, centralized corporations are gradually being fractured into smaller and smaller subunits, leading to the formation of new cottage industries. The technology available with Internet, cell phones, and the other host of technological options available allows for smaller and smaller units of business. In the long run these smaller units of business are usually more profitable per unit versus the great monolithic companies, which tend to become overly bureaucratic, structured, and regulated.

Finding it difficult to adapt, larger, older companies can become economic dinosaurs. So, the fracturing of American business into smaller and smaller subunits—smaller and smaller independent businesses—is a great part of the future of America. *Decentralization* is the byword of the hour.

We should do everything in our power in the political realm, using all of the leverage the government can provide—and that only the government can provide—through the use of the tax system (tax credits, depreciation, and things of this nature) to *encourage* the formation of small businesses. Indeed, economic studies time after time have conclusively proven that the vast majority (approximately 80 percent) of new job creation comes through small businesses. Yet, small business faces its own challenge for survival as well. And, as someone who has run a small business for more than thirty years, I know the challenges well.

The two largest of these multiple obstacles are shortages of capital and expertise. But more and more, as the turnkey revolution continues changing American business, much of the technology and expertise needed can be purchased through outsourcing. This proliferation of outsourcing allows people access to goods and services they could not have had in the past.

For example, rather than hiring an accountant or bookkeeper to do my payroll, I use a Fortune 500 company that does the payroll for me much more competitively than I could pay someone by the hour to do it. The economies of scale available through the *specialization* that is occurring as American businesses fracture into smaller and smaller subunits is something we should encourage. All politicians of all parties should get behind it.

If the Democrats truly want to help the little guy, the best way to do so is encouraging small business formation. Go into underdeveloped geographic zones or impoverished areas of the country, go into urban areas, and set up *free enterprise zones*. Use tax credits to create small businesses and help them thrive. The small businessmen in those areas will work to survive, prosper, and grow and will bring dignity, responsibility, and a productive work ethic to their communities.

Generally speaking, the higher the percentage of people who have ownership in our society (both of the use of the tools for production as well as labor), the more society will grow over the long run—and the more prosperity results. We should use the government to encourage responsible behavior and the use of free enterprise to tackle social problems, not allowing government dependency to attempt to solve them.

As most know, government dependency does not work in the long run. One of the primary roles of the government should be acting as referee. It should ensure that everybody is being treated fairly within the system, as well as encouraging the *growth* of the system from the small-business perspective.

What about solutions for Social Security and Medicare? In the short run these are difficult topics. I don't want to put forth either *doom-and-gloom* or *Cassandra-type* projections based on current trends. In the first place, straight-line projections over the long term based on current trends almost always go awry. Second, if you take the present Social Security and Medicare systems and structures and project them into the future without reform, the programs cannot be sustained.

Reform is going to *have* to take place in order for the systems to *survive*. Tackling the current prognosis on Social Security and Medicare can become extremely gloomy and depressing. Since a number of other books have already taken on this topic, we will not tackle it here.

Why will Russia come to Israel? Let's take a look at some of the reasons for Russia's interest in dominating Israel.

1. Russia will come to Israel because they need a warm-water entrance into the oceans of the world. The Middle East offers that. Russia, under Vladimir Putin's leadership, made a $50 billion oil contract with the late Saddam Hussein and allowed Russian scientists to direct Iran's nuclear weapons programs to destroy Israel. Putin is the former director of the KGB who removed the democratic process from Russia and, at the same time, charmed the West into neutrality.

2. Russia needs oil to regain its military superpower status. Russia hungers for Arabian oil. They must have it to regain their global status, which they lost in the crash of the former Soviet Union.

3. The mineral deposits in the Dead Sea are so great they can't be properly appraised on today's market. It is estimated that the Dead Sea contains two billion tons of potassium chloride, which is potash needed to enrich the soil that is rapidly being depleted around the world. The Dead Sea also contains twenty-two billion tons of magnesium chloride and twelve billion tons of sodium chloride. The wealth of the Dead Sea has the Russian bear salivating at the mouth.

—JOHN HAGEE, *Earth's Final Moments*

I am not necessarily part of the political process at this point. I am primarily trying to help individuals with their personal financial planning and investments. There are plenty of other people who are already working to do that (for example, Pete Peterson's group, The Concord Coalition). The bottom line is that there is great room for optimism and hope—but not without major reform. We will not get through the Social Security and Medicare mazes without some pain. Pain is inevitable, but as a long-term optimist, I know that pain can create great good.

Without the pain of the Revolutionary War, America would never have been born. Without the pain of Valley Forge, George Washington's army would never have been strong enough to defeat the British. Without the pain of the Civil War in the 1860s, slaves would never have been freed, and the beginnings of freedom from oppression for an entire culture in the United States would never have taken place.

Without the pain of the civil rights movement of the 1960s, it is unlikely that blacks in America would have achieved the economic independence that many have. Without the pain of World War I and World War II, freedom would not have survived. Had the Japanese and Hitler's Nazism conquered the world, human oppression would likely have gone to levels never before seen in world history. Through great personal and national sacrifice, these forces were defeated.

The pain of the cold war defeated the Soviet Union and resulted in freedom and prosperity for areas of the world where that never would have been possible. None of the "freedom revolution" that has occurred in many parts of the world would have launched without America being the world's leader in establishing personal and economic freedom.

Although I believe we will see much pain over the next decade or so, I am confident we have the opportunity to create even greater levels of freedom and prosperity in the long run, if we will make the right choices during those periods of pain. These challenges have the ability to create great good if we will choose the right answers and avoid wrong ones.

I am continually drawn to a particular principle contained in what—in my opinion—is one of the best business books ever written, *Good to Great*. In Jim Collins' best-selling book, he talks about several of the greatest corporate-growth stories in American history. Previously, Collins and his coauthor had written another best seller, *Built to Last,* a book about the enduring icons of American industry.[7] In it, Collins demonstrated what made these world-class companies great and enduring and what they did to maintain their status.

During a speaking engagement, Collins was challenged in a somewhat tongue-in-cheek way by the CEO of a corporation, who basically told him, "The information you are giving us is, of course, useless information."

This naturally took Collins back a bit, and he asked, "What do you mean by that?"

The CEO's response indicated that Collins had told the audience what those companies were like today but not how they got there. He hadn't told the listeners or readers how these companies went from being good, publicly-traded companies to being great companies. This so sparked Collins's interest that he undertook a six-year-long study and entered Stanford Business School's MBA program, to discover how companies went from good to great.[8]

The criteria he used for *Good to Great* included the requirement that a corporation be publicly traded (to allow Collins and his research team ready access to the data they needed). In addition, the corporation's stock had to outperform the S&P 500 by at least a three-to-one margin for a minimum of fifteen years, thus superseding most CEO's duration in office.

In a study of companies involving nearly fifty years' worth of data going back to the 1950s, Collins came up with only eleven companies that exhibited these characteristics. After isolating the test cases, he and the students at Stanford then studied what made these companies truly great—what made these companies go from good publicly-traded companies to truly great publicly-traded companies, some of the best the world has ever seen.

They attempted to boil it down to the most common traits

or characteristics. Among them were The Stockdale Paradox, named for the former military officer held captive for eight years during the Vietnam War. Tortured repeatedly by his captors, he had no reason to believe he would ever taste freedom. Yet, he told Collins, the fellow prisoners who failed to get out were those whose unending optimism resulted in such discouragement they died of a broken heart. His words are *extremely* appropriate for the United States today: "Confront the most brutal facts of your current reality, while, at the same time, retain faith that you will prevail in the end, regardless of the difficulties."[9]

There is no question in my mind that during this demographic winter we will face great challenges. Will we have the intestinal fortitude to face up to those challenges? Will we have the guts to take these challenges head-on, instead of blaming someone else or trying to find a scapegoat? Will we look at the problems that we as a society have created through our own behavior, then look for solutions as to how to fix these problems? Will we refuse to allow ourselves to become overwhelmed with depression, but rather face the future, holding to absolute faith that we will ultimately prevail in the end? Will we conquer these challenges?

I am reminded of one story from my own state's heritage, that of the Alamo. Those of you familiar with the story know that 182 Texas settlers held off more than 5,000 of Santa Anna's best troops for thirteen days in an old Spanish mission that was jerry-rigged into a fort at the last moment. What is not widely understood is that all of the men knew they faced almost certain death yet chose to inflict as much damage as possible upon the enemy's troops before succumbing. And what damage they inflicted: some 1,600 deaths and approximately 500 wounded, a ratio of almost ten-to-one, before the battle ended. All the men of the Alamo, including frontier legends Davy Crockett and Jim Bowie, lost their lives.[10]

Yet the loss to the Mexican army proved so severe—as the fort's commander, Colonel William Barret Travis, predicted—that "the victory will cost the enemy so dear, that it will be worse for him than defeat."[11] Despite their defeat, the men of the Alamo damaged the Mexican army's psyche. So much so several weeks later Sam Houston won the decisive Battle of San Jacinto for Texas's Independence. Houston lost only 9 men versus the Mexican army's 630 in a battle lasting only eighteen minutes.[12]

I hate to say this, but I believe it will take this level of resolve, guts, and courage from many of the people in this country before America emerges from its crucible, but I believe that it will happen. In order to do this, we are going to have to remember the lessons of history. As an unknown philosopher once said, "If we learn anything from history, it is the fact that man learns nothing from history." As philosopher, poet and author George Santayana once observed, "Those who cannot remember the past are condemned to repeat it."[13]

During the struggle to form American society, Scottish professor and historian Alexander Fraser Tytler is credited with the observation: "A democracy cannot exist as a permanent form of government. It can only exist until the voters discover that they can vote themselves largesse [generous gifts] from the public treasury."[14] Ironically, more than two centuries later, America is in the apex of this decision-making process. Over the next fifteen to twenty years it will face this certain choice. Will we, out of our own ignorance and greed, decide to continue benefiting ourselves individually at the expense of society?

To do so would be counterproductive, short-term thinking in which pride, ego, and greed would create disastrous results. Will we as a society face up to the problems that we have created for ourselves? No one created these problems for us; we created them for ourselves. We bought into what, in my opinion, are falsehoods—such as that the world is overpopulated. I believe that it can be demonstrated without question that in the long run societies prosper as they have larger numbers of children, thereby growing both social systems and the economy, which benefits everyone in the long run. Will we indulge in pity-party, victimization, short-term, woe-is-me thinking, which leads nowhere except to more pain? The challenge is ours!

CHAPTER 5

DEVELOP A FORMULA
FOR SUCCESS

By James L. Paris and J.W. Dicks

I T IS INTERESTING to see how much the Bible has to say about planning.

> A wise man thinks ahead; a fool doesn't, and even brags about it!
>
> —PROVERBS 13:16, TLB

If you are among the people who have suffered through the long-term economic impacts of the real estate crash of 2008, you may be facing a financial crisis. To climb out of the mess, you must have a plan. Most people we talk with about creating a plan to overcome their crisis say, "I never considered that." For some reason many people believe that planning is for building, but somehow that rebuilding does not also require a plan.

Years ago we liked to watch the old TV program, *MacGyver*. The series offered instructions on problem solving that are still relevant today. We were always amazed to see MacGyver escape from near death each episode with a brilliant use of his resources. Whatever the crisis, MacGyver seemed to escape unharmed. After watching several episodes you would expect to grow bored—but no! MacGyver may be trapped in the back of a shipping truck with a hanger, a bottle of bleach, and a ten-speed bike.

You may ask, "How can any of that help?"

In minutes MacGyver could take apart the bike, use the pipes and bleach to make a bomb, and then light a match attached to the end of the unfolded hanger to ignite the explosion to release himself.

Many who are reading these words possess the resources necessary to solve your problem. The question is: Are you willing to create a plan and use the resources at your disposal to solve the problem? Many times the answer is "no."

Years ago we published a series of books; their common theme was "the thirty-day quick start." We offered a thirty-day program on numerous subjects, such as taxes, investing, and even starting a small business. In retrospect we feel these books were successful because they created a step-by-step plan to accomplish a goal in thirty days. Progress is made each day until after thirty days—success! Just like the old vaudeville joke—"How do you eat an elephant? One bite at a time"—one must solve a crisis one step at a time.

FOUR STEPS TO CREATING YOUR PLAN

1. Prioritize.

2. Create a timeline.

3. Create a daily action plan.

4. Monitor the plan.

Prioritize

As you create your plan, it is crucial to prioritize. Most people are guilty of focusing their energies on the *urgent* rather than the *important*. The late Stephen R. Covey, whose book *The Seven Habits of Highly Effective People* has sold more than twenty-five million copies, put forth this concept as the foundation of his book.

The most common example of this conflict is the telephone. Imagine you are getting ready to create a plan to solve your crisis. You are in a quiet place at home, focusing your thoughts. Yet just as you get ready to type out some of your musings, the telephone rings. Do you run to the phone, only to waste precious time warding off a telemarketer or a friend who just wants to chat? Which activity ranked first in importance: creating your plan or answering the phone?

Too often the most important activities are the least urgent. Essentially the high-priority items don't scream for attention. Yet you must not let the *urgent* take precedence over the *important*. In just about every crisis, urgent issues seem to overshadow the important. Don't fall prey to the temptation to become engrossed in trying to solve short-term symptoms of a long-term problem. Focus your attention on the real problem.

Create a timeline

After determining what is important and developing a plan to address it, the next step is to commit to a schedule to reach your goal. One of the best definitions we have heard for a goal is "a dream with a date for achievement." For example, say you are unemployed. Your goal may be to find a job in thirty days. Perhaps you are starting a new business. Your goal may be to turn a profit within one year.

Create a daily action plan

The best example we can think of is our opportunity over the years to manage salespeople. We determined long ago that sales can be determined mathematically. For example, if you determine that one of every ten people you give a sales presentation to will buy your product and you need to make three sales per day, what do you do? Simple. Make thirty presentations a day. We believe strongly in creating a daily action plan to overcome your crisis. The tendency is to become depressed and actually make less effort than in normal circumstances.

After seeing us glide through a crisis, people often ask, "How do you stay so focused?"

"Don't let the little things bother you," we respond. "And the way we see it, everything is a little thing." Not getting sidetracked emotionally has made problem solving an easier task.

Monitor the plan

It is important to monitor your plan. In many ways it is just as important as creating it. To monitor your plan is essentially to track the progress of your actions. For most people, the best way to do this is through some form of a daily diary or log book. Monitoring both actions and results is imperative.

We have always made a commitment to meet at least once each month to review the progress of our companies. At these meetings we look at the financial statements and also review the ongoing goals of the organization. This month-by-month monitoring has been a great tool in our growth of dozens of businesses.

SEEK COUNSEL OF THE WISE

Once you have drawn up your plan and taken steps to follow it, don't be embarrassed to ask for advice if you stumble somewhere along the way. Just as Mary, the mother of Jesus, asked for His help when the wedding party ran out of wine, we must also ask for help when we need it. Mary could have avoided requesting aid by using a variety of excuses: Why ask for His help? He must already know we are out of wine. He won't want to help solve this problem.

Asking for help is sometimes difficult to do. We often refer to our office phone line as a "financial 911" because of the problems that constantly flow into our switchboard. We often wonder how many other people have problems and do not ask for help.

Whatever the reason, Ezekiel portrays Russia as being in complete command. Why? Because the defender of Israel, the God of Abraham, Isaac, and Jacob, has a hook in Russia's jaw, dragging it into Israel for the greatest object lesson the world has ever seen.

There is comfort and consolation in Ezekiel's prophetic portrait of the world tomorrow. The message is that God is in total control of what appears to be a hopeless situation for Israel. He has dragged these anti-Semitic nations to the nations of Israel to crush them so that the Jews of Israel as a whole will confess that He is the Lord. America and Europe will not save Israel—God will!

—JOHN HAGEE, *Earth's Final Moments*

You may have heard the funny—yet thought-provoking—story about the man who heard of a flood sweeping through the countryside. Concerned over his lack of transportation to a safe place, he prayed. God told him not to fear, He would save the man. No sooner did the man stop praying when a car drove up and the driver offered him transportation to safety.

Surprisingly, the man said, "No, thanks, God will deliver me."

By now falling even harder, the rain steadily flowed until it flooded the first floor of his house. About an hour later a neighbor in a rowboat paddled to the second-story window and offered help.

Again the fellow said, "No, thanks, God will deliver me."

Finally, with water over the roof of his house, the man climbed on to the chimney and clung to the side. A helicopter flying overhead dropped down with a ladder. To the pilot's surprise, the man again refused help, insisting, "God will deliver me." Minutes later, the man drowned.

In heaven the man asked God why he had drowned and the Lord didn't deliver him as He had promised him.

God replied, "I sent a car, a boat, and finally a helicopter, and in each case you refused My help!"

We always think of this story when we hear about people who do not accept assistance from others. For example, one time an older couple asked us to help their daughter. We asked them why she was not asking for herself.

"She has numerous problems," they said, "but she doesn't seem to be willing to accept help."

Obviously we could not give this woman help until she was ready to ask for—and receive—it.

> So I say to you: Ask and it will be given to you; seek and you will find; knock and the door will be opened to you. For everyone who asks receives; the one who seeks finds; and to the one who knocks, the door will be opened. Which of you fathers, if your son asks for a fish, will give him a snake instead?...If you then, though you are evil, know how to give good gifts to your children, how much more will your Father in heaven give the Holy Spirit to those who ask him!
> —LUKE 11:9–11, 13, NIV

This is an incredible section of Scripture to review. The most interesting observation is all the action—seek, knock, ask. The notion of sitting back and waiting for a solution is clearly eliminated here.

FIVE PLACES TO GO FOR HELP

1. God

2. Your pastor

3. Fellow church members

4. Family members

5. Friends

We believe in the truth of Romans 8:28: "In all things God works for the good of those who love him, who have been called according to his purpose" (NIV). The major principle to be gleaned from this verse is that, regardless of how bad things are, there is a purpose for what is happening, and God will bring good from bad circumstances.

Let's say, for example, that you are in need and have never asked "anybody for anything," as the old saying goes. Because of your crisis, for the first time you ask for someone else's help. The process of overlooking your pride and asking for help may have been the character-building experience God had planned for you.

The world is heading toward God's second object lesson. Ezekiel makes it clear that God will send an earthquake that will swallow up the enemies of Israel, just as an earthquake swallowed up the enemies of Moses.

God will use the sword of brother against brother as the second weapon of war. When God sent Gideon to destroy the Midianites, Gideon commanded his meager fighting force of three hundred men to sound the trumpets and to break the pitchers. The Midianites turned their swords against each other in massive confusion and slaughtered one another. (See Judges 7.)

God will bring this battle-tested tactic to wage war against Russia and its allies when they come against Israel. God will cause confusion to come among them as they turn and fight each other, slaughtering each other in history's greatest demonstration of friendly fire.

—JOHN HAGEE, *Earth's Final Moments*

Additionally, personal crisis has produced some of the greatest ministers and counselors alive. As an example, former prisoners have started prison ministries. The most notable is Prison Fellowship, the flourishing organization founded by the late Charles Colson—the one-time White House aide who served time in prison for his role in the 1970s Watergate scandal.

Individuals abused as children have pioneered child abuse protection programs; many other examples abound. We call these great ministers "empathizers." Sympathy is understanding how someone feels, but empathy is experiencing their feelings with them. Be open-minded for the solution to your problem.

> One day Peter and John were going up to the temple at the time of prayer—at three in the afternoon. Now a man who was lame from birth was being carried to the temple gate called Beautiful, where he was put every day to beg from those going into the temple courts. When he saw Peter and John about to enter, he asked them for money. Peter looked straight at him, as did John. Then Peter said, "Look at us!" So the man gave them his attention, expecting to get something from them.
>
> Then Peter said, "Silver or gold I do not have, but what I have I give you. In the name of Jesus Christ of Nazareth, walk." Taking him by the right hand, he helped him up, and instantly the man's feet and ankles became strong."
>
> —ACTS 3:1–7, NIV

What is interesting in this passage from Acts is that Peter and John did not give the man money as he requested. Instead, empowered by the Holy Spirit, they offered him healing.

Instead of meeting his short-term need (money), they met his greater need (health). Don't limit God by expecting Him to meet your financial need only through a downpour of money from heaven!

I remember a man who once came to us for counseling because he could not find a job. He described his situation as desperate and stated he had interviewed all over town and could not even get hired at a convenience store. We asked him to come to our office as if he were going to an interview—to bring a résumé and dress as he would dress for such an occasion.

To our surprise he showed up in a tattered golf shirt, wearing his hair long and dirty, and carrying a difficult-to-read résumé that contained numerous typographical errors. So we bought the man a white dress shirt and a tie, and counseled him about proper appearance and personal presentation during an interview. Several days later he excitedly informed us he had finally landed a job! At first glance money appeared to be the solution to his problem, but simply offering him money wouldn't have addressed the situation.

SIX TYPES OF HELP THAT CAN PROVIDE THE SOLUTION TO YOUR CRISIS

1. Prayer

2. Financial gifts or loans

3. Wise counsel

4. Employment

5. Health

6. Forgiven debts

God has specifically given gifts and abilities to all Christians. One of the most wonderful of these is the gift of giving. Countless Christian brothers and sisters are poised and waiting to meet your needs, if they only knew what they were.

Don't hide your crisis. Let your needs be known. Everyone has times of need, and sharing your crisis situation can put you well on the way to a solution.

REMEMBER: ALL YOU CAN DO IS ENOUGH

There comes a time in your problem-solving process when you have done all that you can do. After you have done everything possible, it is time to rest your mind. Waiting on God to provide can be the most difficult step in the process. The greatest battle in dealing with difficult circumstances is overcoming their emotional stress. Knowing when to stop, relax, and release is crucial.

Please don't misunderstand our message. We are not advocating a lazy, lackluster effort to solve your problems, but there comes a time when you need to stop and recharge your batteries.

> Those who hope in the LORD will renew their strength. They will soar on wings like eagles; they will run and not grow weary, they will walk and not be faint.
>
> —ISAIAH 40:31, NIV

> Be still, and know that I am God.
>
> —PSALM 46:10, NIV

During this period of rest many ideas will come to you, and your solution will become clearer. There is no doubt that God still speaks to us today. The only question is, *Are we listening?* Sadly, for many people, prayer is a one-sided activity. They talk, and God listens. However, this quiet time of relaxation is the perfect opportunity to let God speak while we listen—a new exercise for most of us.

Both of us have had incredible ideas for solutions to problems while walking down the beach, driving in the car, or working around the house. God may wonder why people don't take the time to stop and listen more often.

FOUR WAYS TO RELAX

1. Prayer
2. Family time
3. Exercise
4. Travel

Prayer

Many Middle-Eastern religions practice meditation and claim that it causes great mental rejuvenation. Although this chapter is not intended to be a theological discussion on meditation, we do know that prayer is a great reliever of stress. Setting a time for daily Bible reading and prayer is not just a good thing to do spiritually, but it also provides a means of resting physically and emotionally.

Prayer is not for God's benefit; it is for yours. Some people view Christianity as a list of "dos" and "don'ts." What many have learned through personal tragedy is that the "dos" and "don'ts" are not for God's benefit but for ours. The greatest relief from stress comes through getting to know our Creator and understanding His will for our lives.

Family time

Both of us were blessed with a loving spouse and two children. Even though our children are grown, family time is still important to us. In times of waiting for an answer, a great stress reliever is spending time with our loved ones. Whether it's building with blocks or playing catch, children seem to know how to conquer stress (until they figure out there is an opposite sex!).

We have also learned that talking through the situation with a spouse can be great therapy. More than anything, this is not a time to lock our families out of our lives. Those who are single can find support from close friends, parents, or other family members.

Exercise

Some years ago we listened to a program about avoiding burnout that placed a great emphasis on exercise. In our opinion exercise is one of the greatest stress releasers we have ever experienced. Whether it is jogging, bike riding, swimming, or aerobics, giving your body a physical workout provides incredible rejuvenation. For some people, just walking a few blocks can significantly reduce their stress levels.

You have probably read stories about people who are fanatics about exercise. Once you experience the mental stress release that physical exercise provides, you will become a fanatic about it too. Interestingly enough, most people going through a crisis actually reduce their physical activity. But reduced physical activity can prompt an endless cycle of depression.

Psychologists say that if you smile when you are sad, you can fool your mind into adopting a happy mood. So if you make exercise an integral part of your relaxation routine, it will soon become a pleasant habit.

Travel

"How can I travel?" you may ask. "I am having a financial crisis!" It can be done—and should be. Travel is part of the therapy.

Over the years both of us have had the opportunity to do a great deal of traveling. Although at times we tired of the "road life," there is something about changing your environment that provides relief from stress. If you cannot afford to stay at a hotel, how about "roughing it" in a tent at a campground? Another option is visiting relatives. Also, many churches offer access to camps or wilderness retreats at low prices. The possibilities are endless, and a change of environment for a day or two can provide enormous benefits.

Long ago we heard a radio interview with the late Tim Hansel, whose many books included *When I Relax I Feel Guilty.* His advice about discovering life's joy came to mind when one of our employees requested a Friday afternoon off to go purchase a Christmas tree. In our memory it was the first time he had ever taken any time off in almost a year of employment. However, when Friday rolled around, he said, "I don't feel right about this. Maybe I should stay and work and forget about a Christmas tree this year."

He was feeling guilty about relaxing. We took care of that. We *made* him leave to meet his family and get his Christmas tree.

Thus the heavens and the earth were completed.... By the seventh day God had finished the work he had been doing; so on the seventh day he rested from all his work."
—Genesis 2:1–2, NIV

Just as our Creator rested when the job was done, we must also rest when our work is completed.

CHAPTER 6

EXPECT MIRACLES

By James L. Paris and J. W. Dicks

MANY PEOPLE IN the midst of financial crisis hope for a miracle. They spend hours of time thinking, "If only [whatever it might be] would happen, my problems would be solved." How close they are, but yet so far.

Hope is good. But hope plus belief equals faith, and faith is what delivers.

> Truly I tell you, if you have faith and do not doubt, not only can you do what was done to the fig tree, but also you can say to this mountain, "Go, throw yourself into the sea," and it will be done. If you believe, you will receive whatever you ask for in prayer.
> —MATTHEW 21:21–22, NIV

Aren't these words from Christ a powerful statement for your life? Jesus is telling you the specific answer to your problem. He even highlights it with *"Truly I tell you."*

If you believe (and you must truly believe it in your very soul), God will answer your prayers. Now before you jump up and start praying for a million dollars, let's put it all in perspective. For prayer to work, your heart must be right. Anyone who would simply wish for a million dollars obviously doesn't have his heart where it ought to be, and it is doubtful the money would be forthcoming. However, if your heart is right and you believe, then your prayer will be answered. The key word here is *answer.*

When we think of faith and belief, we are reminded of the story of Jairus, a ruler in Jesus's time. Jairus's problem was one of the most dreaded, the greatest fear of almost every parent: his daughter was dying.

Jairus exemplified faith. He pleaded with the master simply to come and place His hands on the child, knowing that if He did so she would live. Jesus agreed to go with him to his home. Sadly, as they approached the house, men rushed outside to break the news. Jairus was too late. His daughter was dead.

The third weapon in God's arsenal is great hailstones, fire, and brimstone. Two of the most infamous cities that ever existed in history were the cities of Sodom and Gomorrah. Why are they famous? Their fame arises from the fact that they no longer exist. These are the two cities where God poured out fire and brimstone because of their great sin and iniquity, and they were obliterated from the earth.

To this day geologists have sought to discover the location of Sodom and Gomorrah, but God so completely destroyed them they have never been found. Some speculate that they have been buried beneath the Dead Sea, which would explain the rare sulfuric odor and the taste of the water in the Dead Sea.

When Russia and its allies invade Israel, and America and Europe fail to respond, "He who sits in the heavens shall laugh" (Ps. 2:4, NKJV) as He crushes the Russian-Arab tormenters of the apple of His eye. He will crush them as he crushed Pharaoh,

Haman, and Hitler so that Israel and the world "shall know that I am the LORD" (Ezek. 38:23, NKJV).

—JOHN HAGEE, *Earth's Final Moments*

Can you imagine how Jairus felt? *If only* he had hurried faster. *If only* people had not delayed them on their trip to the house. *If only* Jesus hadn't stopped to heal the woman who touched His coat. (See Mark 5:24–35.) All of these *if only's* might have crossed another person's mind had they found themselves in this position.

At this very moment, however, Jesus gives Jairus the answer to his crisis and ours: "Don't be afraid; just believe" (Mark 5:36, NIV).

Christ responded to Jairus's faith. While others laughed at Jesus when He said, "The child is not dead," Jairus and his wife held firm. Then He took hold of the girl's hand and said to her, "Little girl, I say to you, get up!" (Mark 5:39–41). The girl stood up and began walking.

Faith was rewarded.

If prayer and belief are the answer to our problems, does that mean we should sit idle when we are faced with a problem? We don't think so. Time and time again we are reminded in Scripture that we must seek solutions. We must take actions to move toward answers.

One day Jesus was teaching the people. Multitudes had come from far away to hear what He had to say and to see the healings He performed. You can imagine how crowded it must have been. To compound matters, Jesus was inside the home of a friend. It was in this crowded situation that four men arrived, carrying a paralyzed man on a mat. They wanted desperately to get their friend to Jesus; they knew that if they did so, he would be healed. Unfortunately they couldn't get through the throng of people.

It is at such a strategic point that many fail. They look at seemingly insurmountable odds and give up in despair. These men did not. Instead, they climbed up on top of the house and literally made a hole in the roof.

Can you imagine the scene below? Jesus was speaking and healing the people around Him, when all of a sudden someone started cutting a hole in the roof. Moments later the man's friends lowered his mat so that the paralyzed man lay right before Jesus. What did Jesus think about the actions of these men? Mark describes His response: "When Jesus saw their faith, he said to the paralytic, 'Son, your sins are forgiven.... Get up, take your mat and go home" (Mark 2:5, 11, NIV).

From this lesson we can conclude that our actions are also an element of success. In fact, if we were to use a formula for observations, we might say that hope + belief = faith + action = results.

Expecting a miracle is not some "pie-in-the-sky, wishing-and-hoping that somehow things will change" kind of exercise. It is only step seven in a seven-step formula for dealing with a financial crisis. It starts with defining the crisis. That means spelling out the specifics of the crisis, as well as steps you can take to resolve it. Every problem contains the key to its own solution.

The second step is to begin with the end in mind. Set goals that will solve your problem and focus on the solution. Keeping your eyes on the road ahead instead of all the problems and distractions of the moment will help you avoid worry and panic.

Maintaining this kind of focus leads to step three: remain calm. Only when you remain calm can you create the habit of overcoming fear. Left unchecked, fear can literally paralyze you and prevent you from moving forward and taking action to resolve your crisis.

We reviewed steps four through six in the previous chapter, but to summarize:

✕ Step 4: Develop your own success formula. Research and gather facts.

✗ Step 5: Seek counsel of the wise. Pray and ask for guidance.

✗ Step 6: Remember: All you can do is enough. Release your worry to the Lord.

Now, as you complete the final step and expect a miracle, apply the formula of faith: hope + belief = faith + action = results. It is our hope that you face no serious financial crisis. However, by practicing these seven steps, you will be armed to help yourself or anyone else who finds themselves faced with these or other similar misfortunes. Just as with CPR medical training, even though you hope you will never need to use it, it is comforting to know you can if the need arises.

CHAPTER 7

ACTIVATE THE BLESSINGS OF GOD

By Bill Wiese

ONE OF THE things my wife, Annette, and I do is pray and read the Bible daily. This is not to sound over-spiritual, but this is necessary for anyone to have a blessed life. Psalm 119:97 says, "O how I love thy law! It is my meditation all the day" (NKJV). We also speak out Scripture over ourselves and trust God for His Word to take place in our lives. This takes some effort to speak them out of our mouths daily, but God instructs us to meditate in His Word day and night (Deut. 6:1–9; Josh. 1:8; 1 Tim. 4:13–15).

We must speak His Word. Mark 11:23 says, "Whosoever shall *say...*" (KJV, emphasis added). Hebrews 4:14 says, "Let us hold fast our *profession*" (KJV, emphasis added). Joel 3:10 states, "Let the weak *say*, I am strong" (KJV, emphasis added). Deuteronomy 6:7 says, "...and shalt *talk* of them [referring to God's words mentioned in verse 6] when thou sittest in thine house, and when thou walkest by the way, and when thou liest down, and when thou risest up" (KJV, emphasis added).

It even goes on to say for us to place it in front of our eyes, and on our doorposts, and our gates, and on our hand. Proverbs 4:21 says, "Let them [His words] not depart from thine eyes" (KJV).

Speaking out His Word and praying continuously is what we are instructed to do (Ps. 119:62, 97; 1 Thess. 5:17).

If we are trusting in God for our health, then we first ask Him. Then we speak out many of those verses that promise us healthy lives. If it's for our finances, we find God's promises for our provision. If it's for more wisdom, protection, or whatever the case, there are verses to stand on. We have to find the verses and speak them over our lives and not speak the problem. Do we truly value His Word to the point where we will expect to receive what His Word declares? Here are some more verses to give you an idea:

> But thou shalt remember the LORD thy God: for it is he that giveth thee power to get wealth, that he may establish his covenant.
> —DEUTERONOMY 8:18, KJV

> Riches and honour come of thee.
> —1 CHRONICLES 29:12, KJV

> As long as he sought the LORD, God made him to prosper.
> —2 CHRONICLES 26:5, KJV

> If they obey and serve him, they shall spend their days in prosperity, and their years in pleasures.
> —JOB 36:11, KJV

> For thou, LORD, wilt bless the righteous; with favour wilt thou compass him about as with a shield.
> —PSALM 5:12, KJV

> My son, forget not my law; but let thine heart keep my commandments: For length of days, and long life, and peace, shall they add to thee.
> —PROVERBS 3:1–2, KJV

He blesseth the habitation of the just.
—PROVERBS 3:33, KJV

Attend to my words....For they are life unto those that find them, and health to all their flesh.
—PROVERBS 4:20–22, KJV

For by me thy days shall be multiplied.
—PROVERBS 9:11, KJV

The fear of the LORD tendeth to life...he shall not be visited with evil.
—PROVERBS 19:23, KJV

My people shall dwell in a peaceable habitation, and in sure dwellings.
—ISAIAH 32:18, KJV

Honour thy father and thy mother...that it may be well with thee.
—EPHESIANS 6:2–3, KJV

Grace be unto you, and peace, from God our Father, and from the Lord Jesus Christ.
—PHILIPPIANS 1:2, KJV

And the Lord shall deliver me from every evil work.
—2 TIMOTHY 4:18, KJV

There are verses to stand on, even for the different parts that make up our body, such as our hair, teeth, eyes, skin, legs, stature, and so forth. Here are some examples:

× Deuteronomy 34:7 says, "His [Moses's] eye was not dim, nor his natural force abated" (KJV). We don't confess things like our eyes are going bad as we get older, and we are just not as strong as we used to be. No, we say the opposite as in Joel 3:10, "Let the weak say, I am strong."

× Joshua 14:10–11 says, "I am this day fourscore and five years old [eighty-five]. As yet I am as strong this day as I was in the day that Moses sent me [forty-five]" (KJV). Caleb is stating he felt as strong at eighty-five as he did at forty-five years old. We also declare this, since God is no respecter of persons.

× Job 11:15, 17 says, "For then shalt thou lift up thy face without spot...and thine age shall be clearer than the noonday" (KJV). We declare we have clear, healthy skin.

× Solomon wrote, "His locks [hair] are bushy, and black as a raven.... His eyes are as the eyes of doves by the rivers of waters, washed with milk, and fitly set.... His legs are as pillars of marble [strong].... Thy hair is as a flock of goats [thick].... Thy teeth are as a flock of sheep....and there is not one barren among them.... Thine eyes like the fishpools in Heshbon.... This thy stature is like to a palm tree [upright, tall and straight]" (Song of Sol. 5:11–12, 15; 6:5–6; 7:4, 7, KJV). We declare these verses believing in faith that we are not going to get hunched over and decrepit as we age.

× Hebrews 1:3 says, "[The Son] upholding all things by the word of his power...." (KJV). We declare that God upholds all things, including our health.

USING GOD'S WORD TO SPEAK BLESSINGS OVER MY BUSINESS

My wife and I truly value God's Word and love finding these treasures. There are many verses the Lord taught me in regard to prospering my business, such as some of what we just read. I began to declare what His Word said about me and not how I felt. Throughout my real estate career, I had worked a particular tract of homes where we resided. I listed 78 percent of all the properties that came available during that thirty-year period. I also sold 80 percent of my own listings. The average statistic is 2 percent. In other words, the chances of selling the home you list would be extremely rare, as there are so many agents in the MLS system. In addition, I sold 75 percent of the other agents' listings.

These percentages are impossible without adhering to God's principles. Ask any agent, and he or she will tell you that it is unheard of and that I am probably exaggerating. But we have the records to prove it. This is not to brag on myself, by any means, but to boast on what the Lord has done. (See Jeremiah 9:24.)

As we enter the twenty-first century, the State of Israel has now been gathered by the mighty right hand of God and flourishes as the only democratic society in the Middle East. How are we to treat the promises of God toward Israel and the Jewish people? Some evangelicals teach that God has replaced Israel. This is an anti-Semitic theology that refuses to believe God still has a place in His heart for Israel and the Jewish people. Something that has been replaced vanishes and is no longer heard of. It becomes extinct, just as Sodom and Gomorrah are eternally buried. How can something that's been replaced be functioning with such dynamic force and vitality? The nation of Israel dominates the news.

—JOHN HAGEE, *Earth's Final Moments*

When I first started, I felt strongly impressed by the Lord to march around the neighborhood that I was going to work once a day for six days, and seven times on the seventh day. I did what Joshua 1:3 mentions: "Every place that the sole of your foot shall tread upon, that have I given unto you" (KJV). I prayed and fasted during those seven days. When I obtained my first listing, I prayed over the file, asked the Lord for the buyer, and thanked Him every day for sending that buyer to me. I continued doing this for the entire thirty-year period. There were many other things He taught me to do, and as a result I had become the most successful agent in the area. This is all because of Him. I could never have accomplished this on my own. His Word declares that everything I would set my hand to do would prosper, and all that I undertake He would command the blessing upon me (Deut. 28).

Of course, I had to do my part and be diligent to work. I learned good work habits and developed discipline early in life. When I was a young teen, one of my first jobs was as a busboy at a very busy restaurant located right on the ocean in Lauderdale-by-the-Sea, Florida. I used to go in an hour early to make sure my station was set up and ready to go. I stayed after hours to get ready for the next day. While I didn't get paid for this extra preparation, I did this for two years. Well, I was promoted to manager of the busboys and waitresses. Not a big position? It was when you consider I was only fifteen years old. And I got a raise. I found out that if you go the extra mile, you will never have to ask for a raise.

WHAT IS BIBLICAL PROSPERITY?

The biblical definition of prosperity is "always having all sufficiency in all things." It is God's grace abounding toward us.

> And God is able to make *all* grace abound toward you; that ye, *always* having *all* sufficiency in *all* things, may abound to *every* good work.
> —2 CORINTHIANS 9:8, KJV, EMPHASIS ADDED

Having all sufficiency in all things is a guarantee if we serve Him. The mature apostle (John) wrote, "Beloved, I wish above *all* things that thou mayest prosper and be in health, even as thy soul prospereth" (3 John 2, KJV, emphasis added). He wished it above everything else.

God is not opposed to His people having prosperity, but He is *opposed to covetousness* (to lust after, excessively desirous and greedy). First Timothy 6:10–11 states, "For the love of money is the root of all evil: which while some coveted after, they have erred from the faith, and pierced themselves through with many sorrows. But thou, O man of God, flee these things; and follow after righteousness, godliness, faith, love, patience, meekness" (KJV) Money is not the evil, but the love of it that crosses the line into sin.

Part of our good fight of faith (v. 12) is to follow after righteousness and not to lust after money. If we will keep our focus on eternal things and serve God, His desire is for us to prosper.

Prosperity only comes through obedience to His Word. There are those who think if you talk of prosperity that you are being materialistic. Yet, how hypocritical, as everyone goes to work each day to earn money and desires to pay their bills. It is usually the poor or those who are barely making it who will criticize the more affluent. I'm not saying that if you are poor, you are not spiritual. However, you may be simply unaware of God's promises to us. The poor should never be criticized but instead helped. If you are barely making it, then you cannot be a financial blessing to anyone. You would be selfish if all you cared about is your needs. You can be poor and yet have a lust for money, and you can be wealthy and have no lust whatsoever for money.

Dr. C. Thomas Anderson states, "People who work hard for barely an adequate paycheck and who get upset if it is a few dollars short are allowing that paycheck to control their lives. Even though such people might say that money doesn't matter, their behavior says otherwise. They devote great amounts of energy and time to their paycheck.... God is interested in the intent of the heart. It is the love of money that is evil, not money itself."[1]

HAVING THE FAVOR OF GOD

God wants us to have influence in this world so we can bring more souls into His kingdom. The more influence we have, the more souls won. The scripture in Romans 5:17 states, "They which receive abundance of grace and of the gift of righteousness shall reign in life by one, Jesus Christ" (KJV). God's desire is for us to reign in life. What does that mean?

Dr. Theo Wolmarans said, "The Greek word 'reign' in this verse is Strong's No. 936 and other translations of this word in English are: to rule, to reign in life like a king. Clearly God desires to give you tremendous influence in this life so you can influence people toward Heaven. If they aren't saved, you can influence them to salvation. If they are believers, you can encourage them to achieve greater exploits for God's Kingdom. The more influence you have, the more people you can help."[2]

It is our responsibility to appropriate all we can from the Word in order to be the most effective people we can be for His kingdom. Look at these verses, and you will see that we can have favor with God and men, but again, it is not automatic. We have to do something:

> And Jesus increased in wisdom and stature, and in favour with God and man.
>
> —LUKE 2:52, KJV

Notice, as He increased in wisdom, Jesus found favor with His Father and those around Him.

> Let not mercy and truth forsake thee...so shalt thou find favour and good understanding.
>
> —PROVERBS 3:3–4, KJV

Being merciful and truthful is a condition for obtaining favor.

> Blessed is the man that heareth me, watching daily at my gates, waiting at the posts of my doors. For whoso findeth me findeth life, and shall obtain favour with the Lord.
> —PROVERBS 8:34–35, KJV

Again, finding God's favor means being able to receive instruction.

> He that diligently seeketh good procureth favour.
> —PROVERBS 11:27, KJV

> Good understanding giveth favour.
> —PROVERBS 13:15, KJV

> The king's favour is toward a wise servant.
> —PROVERBS 14:35, KJV

> Whoso findeth a wife...obtaineth favour.
> —PROVERBS 18:22, KJV

If we "get understanding," we will find favor. How do we "get understanding"?

> Through thy precepts I get understanding.
> —PSALM 119:104, KJV

> He that heareth reproof getteth understanding.
> —PROVERBS 15:32, KJV

It always comes back to us being able to receive instruction from God's Word and obeying it. In addition, I definitely found more favor since I met my beautiful wife (Prov. 18:22). I know it is because of her that my life has been especially blessed.

FAITH

Faith is one of the most important topics in the entire Bible for these reasons:

1. Jesus will be looking for faith (Luke 18:8).

2. We walk by faith (2 Cor. 5:7).

3. We live by faith (Gal. 3:11).

4. We are saved through faith (Eph. 2:8–9).

5. We can't please God without faith (Heb. 11:6).

Everyone's faith is at a different level, and our faith needs to be exercised. We have all been given a "measure of faith" (Rom. 12:3, MEV). No one is given a greater amount. We all start off with the same amount. Where is your faith now?

1. No faith (Mark 4:40)

2. Weak in faith (Rom. 4:20)

3. Little faith (Matt. 6:30)

4. Shipwrecked faith (1 Tim. 1:19)

5. Don't know where your faith is (Luke 8:25)

6. Strong faith (Rom. 4:20)

7. Great faith (Matt. 15:28)

8. Unfeigned faith (sincere, genuine, without hypocrisy) (2 Tim. 1:5)

9. Full of faith (Acts 6:5)

Three of the ingredients of faith are as follows:

1. Love. Galatians 5:6 says, "Faith which worketh by love" (KJV). First Corinthians 13:2 states, "And though I have all faith, so that I could remove mountains, and have not charity [love], I am nothing" (KJV). If we have no love, our faith is void. A requirement for faith to work is for us to walk in love.

2. Patience. James 1:3 states, "That the trying of your faith worketh patience" (KJV; see also Romans 5:3; Hebrews 6:12; 10:36; James 1:4; 5:7, 10–11; 2 Peter 1:6; Revelation 3:10; 13:10.) If we have little or no patience, then we can have little or no faith. God also has all patience (Rom. 15:5; Col. 1:11; Rev. 1:9). We will have many tests to develop our patience. This is what separates the men from the boys, so to speak. Are we committed to stay with it and not waver (James 1:6–8), and not allow doubt to come out of our mouths? Time proves whether we believe God or not.

3. Works. James 2:17 says, "Even so faith, if it hath not works, is dead, being alone" (KJV). James is explaining that if you say to the naked or poor and needy, "Depart in peace, be ye warmed and filled…what doth it profit?" (v. 16, KJV). If you don't give them the money, clothes, or housing, then your faith is dead. Your words mean nothing without your giving. "By works was faith made perfect" (v. 22, KJV).

Who are the allies of Russia who will join them in this unholy war to destroy the nation of Israel and exterminate the Jews? God gives their names and addresses through the prophet Ezekiel.

Persia, Ethiopia, and Libya are with them, all of them with shield and helmet; Gomer and all its troops; the house

of Togarmah from the far north and all its troops—many
people are with you.

—EZEKIEL 38:5–6, NKJV

Persia is modern-day Iran. In recent years, Russia and Iran
have joined forces to create long-range nuclear missiles that can
hit London, Jerusalem, and New York. During the earlier administration of Prime Minister Benjamin Netanyahu, Israeli intelligence gave photographic proof that Russian scientists were
directing and supervising Iran's nuclear weapons programs.

There is no doubt a nuclear collision is coming in the near
future in the Middle East. If Israel bombs Iran's eight nuclear
sites with laser-guided, bunker-buster bombs, it could easily
launch Ezekiel's war, described in Ezekiel 38–39.

—JOHN HAGEE, *Earth's Final Moments*

Faith needs to have corresponding action. Our mouths and
our actions have to show we believe it. Praying for someone who
has no food is not enough. We need to also supply the food for
them. In regard to the believing part, here is an example: Say I
needed ten thousand dollars to pay some bills, and my dad says
he will send me the money by next Friday. If I go around saying,
"I'm worried that we are not going to be able to pay these bills,
and I sure hope we get the ten thousand dollars from Dad," I'm
obviously not trusting that my father will send it. Otherwise I
would be at rest knowing it's coming next Friday, right? We need
to be at rest, trusting God's Word will work for us.

Acts 14:9 states, "…and perceiving that he had faith to be
healed" (KJV). In other words, he had enough faith. But the con-
verse would be, he may not have had enough faith to be healed.
James 1:6–7 says, "But let him ask in faith, nothing wavering…for
let not that man think that he shall receive any thing of the Lord"
(KJV). He just let us know we won't receive if we have any doubt.

How often many of us doubt, and then we wonder why we

haven't received? We become double minded, as in James 1:8. We use the excuse that, "It must not be God's will," rather than admit our faith may not be as developed as it should! You might say, "But Bill, you are placing condemnation on us." No, I'm simply trying to get you to see that our faith needs to be developed. We should be able to admit that we might not yet be strong in faith. When the apostles asked Jesus why they couldn't cast out a devil from a man's son, He said, "Because of your unbelief" (Matt. 17:20, KJV). He didn't pull any punches. He wasn't placing condemnation on them. He just let them know the truth. He wanted them to learn, and that is what we should be willing to do. We should be able to receive correction from His Word. In addition, we should also be willing to receive instruction or correction from our pastors and other godly people in our lives.

Charles Spurgeon said, "Get your friends to tell you your faults, or better still, welcome an enemy who will watch you keenly and sting you savagely. What a blessing such an irritating critic will be to a wise man, what an intolerable nuisance to a fool."[3]

Jesus said over and over, "Your faith hath made you whole." Look at the woman with the issue of blood in Matthew 9:20–22. What about blind Bartimaeus in Mark 10:46–52? What about the man who was let down through the roof in Mark 2:4? What about the woman from Canaan in Matthew 15:22–28? Look at the centurion in Matthew 8:5–10. And look at the story about Jairus's daughter (Mark 5:23). In each case, it was their faith that brought the healing. The woman with the issue of blood didn't even ask Him for her healing. She just said, "If I may but touch his garment, I shall be whole" (Matt. 9:21, KJV). Jesus was pleased with her faith.

I am not talking about having faith in our own faith, but having faith in His faith. It is by the faith *of* Him (Gal. 2:16; 3:22; Eph. 3:12; Phil. 1:27; 3:9; Col. 2:12). We are able to appropriate the blessings of God because of what Jesus has done. It is His faith that obtained the things of God for us. We simply receive them by exercising our faith in what He has done. Our faith is in trusting what He has accomplished.

God is not moved by our whining and begging. To have faith is to show we trust and rely upon Him while not fretting about our circumstances. We simply ask Him in faith, trust Him, and thank Him for the victory. Now, it is obvious throughout the Scriptures we have to ask for things that are scriptural (1 John 5:14). That goes without saying. So how do we acquire faith? It comes by hearing, by reading His Word, by speaking it out of our own mouths, and by listening to good teachings on the subject. There is no other way to acquire faith. Romans 10:17 says, "So then faith cometh by hearing, and hearing by the word of God" (KJV). The reason the Bible says that we can't please God without faith is because God is pleased when He can bless us. His motive in being pleased is not for self-gratification. It is because He is pleased when He can give to us. God's motive is always to give. He can't bless us unless we show Him faith.

HAVE A VISION FOR YOUR LIFE

Every one of us needs to have a vision. The Bible says, "Where there is no vision, the people perish" (Prov. 29:18, KJV). Having a vision is different from setting goals—and we should do that also—but a vision is more of a spiritual direction and plan, where a goal may not be spiritual. A vision is where God is telling you what He sees you accomplishing in your life. It is usually bigger than we would think. If you find out the vision God has for you by praying, you will discover His perfect will for your life. It will be the thing that will fulfill your desires and what He has equipped you for. It will be your destiny.

Jentezen Franklin said, "When you begin to come to your vision, you can almost hear God saying, 'This is the highest you! This is what I see you doing. This is My dream and My vision and My destiny for your life.' It will always be bigger than what you thought you could ever do or be. It will always be impossible to achieve without the continual help of the Holy Spirit. But it is not your idea in the first place. It is His. It is God's idea for you."[4]

GOD'S COVENANT WITH MAN

One last point: God has made a covenant with Abraham, and He blessed him and made him rich (Gen. 12:2–5, 13:1–2, 6; 17:2; 24:35, 53). We are heirs of Abraham (Gal. 3:13–14). We also have what God promised him. Deuteronomy 28 describes in detail the blessings and the curses. It is truly an eye-opener when you see what the curse entails. Basically it is poverty and every sickness and disease—known and unknown. In other words, we do not have to be a part of those curses since we are heirs. God has redeemed us from the curse. How wonderful is that!

CHAPTER 8

HARNESSING THE WISDOM OF GOD

By Bill Wiese

Many years ago I had a profound dream. Recognizing it came from God, I have never forgotten it. In this dream I was in my home. Suddenly I could see right through the walls, and a huge snake pounding on the walls and windows, trying to get in. Approximately a foot in diameter, it was slimy, and green. Though relentless in its attempts to find an opening, I sensed it could not see.

It searched for an opening by pounding all around the closed-up house. Though no windows were open, when I looked at the front door, it didn't reach the floor. It was as if someone had sawed off the bottom six or eight inches. Fear struck; I knew this snake would eventually find the opening. About a half an hour passed in the dream. Sure enough, the snake squeezed under the bottom of the door and tore through the house. Slime covered everything. Frightened, I ran out the back door. Yet once outside I thought, "I need to go back in and get that thing out of my house." As soon as I stepped back inside, I woke up.

Certain this dream came from God, I asked the Lord to show

me its meaning. After praying for a while, I understood. I did not hear an audible voice, but I felt a strong impression and saw clearly. A peace came over me that confirmed the message: the snake was a demonic spirit attempting to get into my house—which represented my life. The evil spirit couldn't see that there were walls, but he knew enough to continue to pound to eventually find an opening. The walls represented the hedge that is around our lives if we live for the Lord and are saved.

In a parable in Mark 12, Jesus said, "A certain man planted a vineyard, and set an hedge about it…" (v. 1, KJV). We know the man in the parable is God, and the vineyard was Israel.[1] God had set a hedge around Israel, and He has set one around us. Ecclesiastes 10:8 says, "Whoso breaketh an hedge, a serpent shall bite him." In Job 1:10 Satan said to God, "Hast not thou made an hedge about him, and about his house, and about all that he hath on every side?" (KJV). So we have a hedge, but we can break it ourselves. My hedge was obviously open, and at the front door.

Now, the front door represented the first thing that would give entry into my life, which was praying and reading God's Word on a daily basis. In other words, the first thing we are to do every morning is worship Him, pray, and read His Word. In Mark 1:35 it states that Jesus "rising up a great while before day, he went out, and departed into a solitary place, and there prayed" (KJV). Ezekiel 12:8 states, "In the morning came the word of the LORD unto me" (KJV). Many other verses state this. (See Job 7:17–18; Psalm 5:3; 57:8; 59:16; 63:1; 78:34; 108:2; Jeremiah 25:3.)

Our reading and praying first thing shows God that He has the first place in our lives. Whenever I missed a day here and there, the crack under the front door widened. So did my hedge. God can also remove our protection if we are in disobedience (Ps. 80:12; 89:40; Isa. 5:5; Mark 12:1). This open hedge invited problems into my life, and it was my fault.

Just prior to my dream, while working out at the gym, someone bumped the weight rack. A five-pound weight fell, hit my big toe, and broke it. I really hurt! I complained to the Lord and said, "Why did this happen? Your Word says no evil shall happen to the just." (See Psalm 54:7; 121:7; Proverbs 11:8; 12:21; 19:23; Ecclesiastes 8:5.) Just days later, I dreamt of that snake. After revealing the interpretation, I believe the Lord said to me, "You had time to go to the gym every day, but not time to pray and read My Word every day." Now God is not the one who caused that weight to fall on my toe. However, we do have an enemy, and there are benefits when we stay under the umbrella of God's protection. I gave place to the devil, which contradicts the Bible's advice (Eph. 4:27). His Word declares that we can be hidden in the secret place, that no evil shall befall us, that we shall not be visited with evil, wickedness shall not afflict us, that not a bone shall be broken, that the enemy shall flee seven ways before us, and so on (Deut. 28:7; Ps. 27:5; 31:20; 34:20; 89:22; 91:1; Prov. 12:21; 19:23). I believe God made it clear to me to read and pray daily as He said in Deuteronomy 6:1–9, Joshua 1:8, and elsewhere.

Some people have told me: "Bill, you are in legalism. You are in bondage. It's legalistic to say we must read and pray daily. You are on a works trip." I understand their thoughts. We can go too far, and no one can keep all the Word. The New Testament says that if we are in works, then we are not under grace. However, our reason for wanting to keep His Word should come from a desire to please Him, not to earn anything. We are to be doers of the Word. This is also not a "works trip" because it does not have to do with my salvation but with my protection.

Look at these three verses:

> O how I love thy law! It is my meditation all the day.
>
> —Psalm 119:97, KJV

> Thank we God without ceasing.
>
> —1 Thessalonians 2:13, KJV

Pray without ceasing.

—1 Thessalonians 5:17, kjv

How many of us do that? If we are told to pray and give thanks without ceasing and to meditate on His Word all day, then why is it legalism to read and pray daily? The Word is clear that we are to stay in obedience if we want the blessings and promises of God (Josh. 1:8; Job 36:11; Ps. 1:1; 37:19; 122:6; Prov. 3:33; 4:5-8; 22:4; 24:4; Eccles. 8:5; Isa. 1:19; Jer. 5:25; Luke 6:35-38; Heb. 11:6; 1 John 3:22). Hebrews 11:6 states, "He is a rewarder of them that diligently seek him" (kjv).

You become legalistic when you think that you are earning your blessings. God gives us the grace to keep His Word and overcome sin. It is not that I feel justified in walking in the blessings because of *keeping* His Word. It is because I desire to show Him I love Him by *obeying* His Word.

I'm sure we all eat food and drink every day, even three times a day. Now would I be justified in saying you were being fanatical for eating every day? Yet Jesus said that His Word is our daily bread (Luke 11:3; John 6:33, 41, 48). He said that man does not live by bread alone but by every Word of God. Reading and praying daily is more important than eating food. It is, again, another place in His Word to obey and see the benefits.

I'm simply sharing what has worked in my life. I have done this for more than thirty-five years since my dream, and He has protected my wife and me faithfully. I have remained healthy and never taken a sick day nor suffered any injuries. It is not because of what we have done, but because He is faithful to keep His Word. Our part is simply to obey and give Him thanks every day (Ps. 61:8; 72:15; 86:3; 119:164; Acts 17:11; 1 Cor. 15:31; 1 John 3:22).

Proverbs 8:34 says, "Blessed is the man that heareth me [wisdom], watching *daily* at my gates, waiting at the posts of my doors" (kjv, emphasis added).

WISDOM: DO YOU HAVE IT?

The *Vine's Expository Dictionary* defines *wisdom* this way: "Insight into the true nature of things, the ability to discern modes of action with a view to their results."

It is the skill to use knowledge and understanding properly. In other words, it is the ability to see truth and the big picture; to know what to do and to know what will be the outcome of a matter. The Bible states that, "The fear of the LORD is the beginning of wisdom" (Prov. 9:10, KJV). Without the fear of the Lord, we don't even have the beginning of wisdom. We might possess some knowledge, but knowledge without wisdom only "puffs up" (1 Cor. 8:1, NKJV). According to God, you cannot even have the beginning of wisdom unless you fear Him. And fearing the Lord is only the beginning. You are to continue to seek to behold His glory and be changed into the same image from glory to glory (2 Cor. 3:18). The purpose is to gain an appreciation and stand in awe of His Word, as it is above even His name (Ps. 138:2).

Colossians 3:16 declares, "Let the word of Christ dwell in you richly in *all* wisdom" (KJV, emphasis added). As you can see from that verse alone, if His Word dwells in us, we will gain wisdom. David said in Psalm 119:98–99, "Thou through thy commandments hast made me wiser than mine enemies.... I have more understanding than all my teachers: for thy testimonies are my meditation" (KJV). Why was David wiser? Because of meditating on God's Word and obeying it.

Except for Jesus, the wisest and wealthiest man who ever lived was King Solomon (1 Kings 3:5–13; 4:29–30; 10:1–7, 23; 1 Chron. 29:25; 2 Chron. 1:1–12, 9:1–6, 22; Eccles. 1:13, 16; 2:12). He said to seek after wisdom; it is the principal thing (Prov. 4:5–8, 8:1–5). So what did this brilliant man, who accomplished more than any other man in history, call important? Reflecting after his life of achievement, he summed it up: "Let us hear the conclusion of the whole matter: Fear God, and keep his commandments: for this is the whole duty of man" (Eccles. 12:13, KJV). That is a short but profound statement!

What does the evolving relationship between Iran and Russia mean for the surrounding Arab nations? They believe the Islamic fanatical vision of exterminating the Jews can be realized with Russia's help. Absolute control of Jerusalem as the capital for the new Palestinian state will be within their grasp.

However, there is one problem looming on the horizon: God Almighty, whom the Russians defy and Islamics denounce, has brought this evil axis of power into Israel to bury it before the eyes of the world. The destruction of Russia and its Islamic allies is going to be the most powerful object lesson the world has seen since Pharaoh and his army were drowned in the Red Sea.

—JOHN HAGEE, *Earth's Final Moments*

Yet, most people do not adhere to his insightful advice (Matt. 7:13–14). Why? Because many have the erroneous idea that the Bible represents rules and restrictions, loss of freedom, and even a life of poverty. Yet the Bible is not a set of restrictive rules; it contains liberating principles. It is not a book of don'ts, but rather a book involving a relationship between God and man. In this relationship His desire is for us to discover His perfect will for our lives, to use our talents and abilities to help spread the gospel, and to feed the poor. He also desires for us to enjoy our life and to celebrate it.

In addition, the Bible is an instruction manual for life's issues. If a mechanic works on a car and never consults the manual, he will make many unnecessary mistakes. The same is true of our lives. If we do not read our manual, the Bible, we will invite *unnecessary* hardships. Adhering to God's principles only enhances our lives. Finding wisdom is more precious than rubies or fine gold (Prov. 3:14–15).

"Wisdom is not a rulebook," says Australian pastor and author Phil Pringle. "She is an attitude guiding how we do life. She rewards with favour, honour and success. Wisdom is to be knowledgeable yet not proud, confident yet not arrogant, nor naïve, but not cynical either, trusting yet not gullible, believing yet proving all things, courageous yet not foolhardy, humble yet not servile, encouraging yet not flattering, profound yet relatable, appropriate, being winsome yet uncompromising, righteous yet not self-righteous, disciplined yet celebrating life, prosperous yet not miserly, generous."[2] I think that sums up wisdom pretty well.

We don't seek wealth; we seek wisdom. There is an earthly wisdom, and there is a godly wisdom. James 3:15 says that earthly wisdom is sensual and devilish. Godly wisdom is "first pure, then peaceable, gentle, and easy to be intreated, full of mercy and good fruits, without partiality, and without hypocrisy" (v. 17, KJV).

To obtain godly wisdom, it first takes a commitment to our Savior, and many will not make that commitment. This is sad, since James 1:5 says that we can simply ask God for wisdom, and He "giveth to all men liberally" (KJV).

Again, God is the one who is always giving. We only have to ask, because Jesus said, "It is your Father's good pleasure to give you the kingdom" (Luke 12:32, KJV), and wisdom is part of the kingdom (1 Cor. 1:30).

One proof you have wisdom is that you will have a desire to win souls to Christ. Proverbs 11:30 states, "He that winneth souls is wise" (KJV). Charles Spurgeon said, "Soul-winning is the chief business of the Christian.... It should be the main pursuit of every true believer."[3]

A wise person is also one who has a desire to understand the things of God and to have a greater knowledge of Him. (See Psalm 119:99, 127–130, 161–162; Proverbs 1:5, 2:1–6.) There are also great benefits to those who have wisdom. Proverbs 3:13–16 states,

"Happy is the man that findeth wisdom, and the man that getteth understanding.... Length of days is in her right hand; and in her left hand riches and honour" (KJV). How is that for a promise?

As a youngster, I watched *Kung Fu*. This TV show always started with a scene where young Caine would wait outside the temple doors in hope to gain admittance to the school. He stayed out there day after day, even in the rain. Finally, one day the master of the school opened the door. Seeing Caine's hunger and commitment, the master knew he was the kind of person they wanted. The same is true of God. He is looking for someone who hungers passionately after His Word. As Proverbs 8:34 says, "Blessed is the man that heareth me [wisdom], watching daily at my gates, waiting at the posts of my doors" (KJV).

Many people make a lifetime commitment of discipline to win in the Olympics or be the best at their sport. They pay a high price. Most things in life that are worth acquiring take discipline, persistence, and dedication. Yet most will not pay the price for the most valuable of all pursuits. King Solomon asked for wisdom and pursued it, and not only did God give him the wisdom, but also wealth came along with it. That is why Proverbs 4:7 says, "Wisdom is the principal thing; therefore get wisdom: and with all thy getting get understanding" (KJV).

These next stories reveal wisdom in some aspect, especially those involving Jesus.

DANIEL'S ATTITUDE IN A REQUEST

In Daniel 1, Daniel and his three friends were told to eat the king's food in order to fatten themselves up before their appearance with the king. Since they had been in prison, they hadn't eaten too well. The king even required the prince of the eunuchs to make sure he fattened them up, or face losing his head (v. 10). However, Daniel didn't want to defile himself with the king's food and purposed himself not to eat it. He asked if he could eat only vegetables. Yet Daniel had to use wisdom, as the man would normally say, "Not even a possibility." So Daniel said, "Prove thy servants, I beseech thee, ten days; and let them give us pulse [vegetables] to eat, and water to drink" (v. 12, KJV).

Two points here:

1. First of all, he asked for only a ten-day trial run, which would leave enough time for the king's food to work if the vegetarian diet didn't. After all, the prince didn't want to lose his head. Daniel showed consideration for him; the prince had three years to fatten them up (v. 5). Daniel also had to have been in a favorable position with the prince of the eunuchs to even ask in the first place (v. 9)—which he had because of his excellent spirit (Dan. 5:12, 14; 6:3).

2. When Daniel asked, he said, "I beseech thee..." he demonstrated a humble attitude. *Beseech* means "please" or "I beg you." All through the Bible the word *beseech* is used by those with a humble attitude. Since Daniel asked with humility and wisdom, the prince granted his request. Consideration of others is showing wisdom.

WISDOM IN CONFRONTATION

This is an excellent story of just how to say something in order for it to be received well. Look at the situation where the prophet Nathan had to tell King David about his sin with Bathsheba.

Instead of telling him straight on, Nathan shared a story that is recorded in 2 Samuel 12:1–7 (KJV):

> There were two men in one city; the one rich, and the other poor. The rich man had exceeding many flocks and herds: But the poor man had nothing, save one little ewe lamb, which he had bought and nourished up: and it grew up together with him, and with his children; it did eat of his

own meat, and drank of his own cup, and lay in his bosom, and was unto him as a daughter. And there came a traveler unto the rich man, and he spared to take of his own flock and of his own herd, to dress for the wayfaring man that was come unto him; but took the poor man's lamb, and dressed it for the man that was come to him. And David's anger was greatly kindled against the man; and he said to Nathan, As the LORD liveth, the man that hath done this thing shall surely die....And Nathan said to David, Thou art the man.

You can see how David would have now been convicted and couldn't brush it off. It would not have been an easy thing to simply walk up to the king and tell him he was in sin, even as a prophet. It took the wisdom of God, but Nathan's presentation left David's heart full of conviction and repentance.

The story of Esther is the most amazing display of God's wisdom in operation. There are too many points to emphasize here, so I encourage you to read the account. It is a marvelous example of how prayer and fasting will bring God on the scene. You will also see how He is well able to reverse some disastrous events from occurring and to see that justice takes place.

THE ANSWERS OF JESUS

Who will cast a stone?

I want to share a few stories of the One who has the ultimate wisdom—Jesus Christ.

John 8 describes a situation where the scribes and Pharisees brought a woman caught in adultery before Jesus. They reminded Him that "Moses in the law commanded us, that such should be stoned: but what sayest thou?" (v. 5, KJV). Since the Law said she should be stoned, they were right. So how would Jesus show mercy to her but not violate His own Word? His ministry was to fulfill the Law, but Jesus always showed mercy to the humble, and He showed forgiveness. How could He accomplish both?

He looked at all those hypocrites who were accusing her and stooped down to write in the sand. Then He stood up and said, "He that is without sin among you, let him first cast a stone at her" (v. 7, KJV). His answer did not violate His established Word, but at the same time, it rose above the Law and brought mercy and forgiveness.

Iran is rapidly developing nuclear weapons to use against Israel and America and is ready to share its nuclear technology with other Islamic nations.... That means every Islamic terrorist organization is going to have the opportunity to use these atomic weapons. Now think about that. That means suitcase bombs could be exploding in several of the major cities of America at the same time. Imagine the chaos and confusion of a dozen Katrinas happening at the same time, created by the devastation of atomic suitcase bombs. Each bomb could kill up to a million people if exploded in a highly populated area like New York City. You say it can't happen. You're exactly wrong. Eugene Habiger, former Executive Chief of Strategic Weapons at the Pentagon, said that an event of nuclear mega-terrorism on US soil is "not a matter of if but when."[4]

—JOHN HAGEE, *Earth's Final Moments*

Christ's wise statement left those men without a demand that the Law be carried out. Their guilt left them speechless and positioned her for mercy. What a display of the wisdom of God in not violating His own Word and yet rising above it. Scholars speculate that He was probably writing their sins on the ground. Those scoundrels were accusing her, when they were worse (Matt. 23:13–33). He shut their mouths. God's awesome wisdom and His obvious disdain for hypocrisy is something to shout about.

Show me a penny!

Another incident occurred in Mark 12:14-17, where the Pharisees and Herodians asked Jesus, "Is it lawful to give tribute to Caesar, or not?" (KJV). They knew that most of the crowd were Jews and didn't like having to pay taxes. If Jesus said to pay it, the crowd would hate Him and not listen to Him. If He told them not to pay it, He could be arrested by the Roman government for promoting tax evasion. They wanted to trap Him, but they didn't know whom they were playing with. Jesus said the famous line, "Render to Caesar the things that are Caesar's, and to God the things that are God's" (KJV). He didn't break the law regarding payment of taxes, but He didn't let those hypocritical religious leaders off the hook either. They themselves were not giving the way they were commanded to in the Scriptures (Matt. 23:14), such as helping and giving to the poor (Matt. 23:2–4). He let them know in a subtle way that they were not so pious. The Jews could more readily accept His statement to pay taxes since He showed them His command to also give to God.

By what authority?

Matthew 21:23–27 describes this encounter with Jesus: "The chief priests and the elders…said, 'By what authority doest thou these things? and who gave thee this authority?' And Jesus answered and said unto them, I also will ask you one thing, which if ye tell me, I in like wise will tell you by what authority I do these things. The baptism of John, whence was it? from heaven, or of men? And they reasoned with themselves, saying, If we shall say, From heaven; he will say unto us, Why did ye not then believe him? But if we shall say, Of men; we fear the people; for all hold John as a prophet. And they answered Jesus, and said, We cannot tell. And he said unto them, Neither tell I you by what authority I do these things" (KJV).

These religious leaders tried to trap Him, and He in turn stopped their mouths. Again, the wisdom of God is astounding!

There are many more stories throughout the Bible that reveal wisdom on how, when, and in what attitude to say a thing.

WISDOM FROM WISE ASSOCIATION

Proverbs 13:20 states that, "He that walketh with wise men shall be wise: but a companion of fools shall be destroyed" (KJV). We can pick up the spirit of wisdom as we associate with wise people and as we stay connected to our all-wise God. Wisdom doesn't come by casual contact. The verse says, "He that walketh…"; that means, day in and day out spending time with those who are wise.

We could look at the relationship of Moses and Joshua. Joshua served Moses for forty years and had a similar anointing. Deuteronomy 34:9 says, "And Joshua the son of Nun was full of the spirit of wisdom; for Moses had laid his hands upon him" (KJV). Look at Elijah and Elisha. Scholars say Elisha served Elijah for between ten and twenty years. Then Elisha saw twice as many miracles (2 Kings 2:9–15). Look at Paul and Timothy. They served together in the ministry, and Timothy benefited from Paul's insight. Paul said Timothy was his "dearly beloved son…the unfeigned faith that is in thee" (2 Tim. 1:2, 5, KJV).

We should desire an opportunity where God arranges a divine connection with someone. Those relationships are extremely beneficial for us. We should choose our friends wisely and be aware of divine connections.

Wisdom is also knowing who you are dealing with and how to handle different people. There are three different types of people in the world, according to leading psychologist and best-selling author Dr. Henry Cloud: "Wise people, foolish people, evil people. Those are the three categories of behavior that you will find yourself dealing with in virtually any situation involving others.…Different people, in different categories, require different strategies."[5] Just as there is a weather satellite to predict the weather, there is a way to predict people. He states, "The satellite that will give you the most accurate predictions is the ability to diagnose character."[6]

We must understand the character of others so we know how to deal with them. You don't handle everyone the same way. Dr. Cloud points out that the key diagnostic of the wise person is: "When truth presents itself, the wise person sees the light, takes it in, and makes adjustments.... The mature person meets the demands of life, while the immature person demands that life meet her demands.... Wise people likewise address their faults, and you see changes in actions and behaviors instead of patterns that go unaffected by the feedback.... The fool does the opposite: he rejects the feedback, resists it, explains it away, and does nothing to adjust to meet its requirements." He goes on to explain evil people, "There are some people whose desire is to hurt others and do destructive things.... This is difficult for some leaders to come to grips with; they think that they can reason with anyone and finally get through. But evil people are not reasonable. They seek to destroy. So you have to protect yourself—ergo, lawyers, guns (police), and money."[7] He summarizes the three:

1. With wise people—Talk to them, give resources, and you will get a return.

2. With foolish people—Stop talking to them about problems; they are not listening. And stop supplying resources; they squander them. Instead, give them limits and consequences.

3. With evil people—You have to go into protection mode, not helping mode, when dealing with evil people.[8]

WISDOM—SEEING THE END RESULT

My brother-in-law, Greg, is a corporate CPA who also advises wealthy clients about their investments. One had purchased land to develop a shopping center, hotel, office buildings, and other facilities. After a year of research, the team of attorneys and Greg completed their feasibility study. All agreed it was a go. Greg informed the owner that he would earn approximately ten million dollars in just one year of operations. They were prepared to proceed, until Greg pulled the owner aside to say: "Mike, you will make ten million, but you are seventy years old, and the project will take five years out of your life. You might not have much longer after that to even enjoy the money, and you already have hundreds of millions. Why not just enjoy these later years with your wife?"

Mike decided Greg was right, and canceled the project. Now Greg would have earned half a million for his share in just the first year alone. But instead of thinking of himself, he thought of Mike and saw the big picture.

The advice to Mike was, first, wise on Greg's part. Second, it reflected the love of God to look out for others even at your own expense. Yes, that is the Golden Rule, which many do not fully understand or follow. John C. Maxwell states, "To many people, the Golden Rule sounds like a soft approach to business. But nothing could be further from the truth.... It really is a win for everybody.... The Golden Rule really does work."[9]

Often, our self-centered lives take precedence over another's needs, and we fail to comprehend that this Golden Rule is actually the law of sowing and reaping. How we treat others will come back on us in this life and in the life to come.

Since he is not focused on money, Greg has been blessed and prosperous throughout his career. This is also due to his wife, his better half, Janice. Greg, like me, also married over his head! Seeing the end result *is* godly wisdom.

WISDOM REVEALS THE ANSWER

I had sold a home, and we were about one month into the escrow period. The preliminary title report showed that the owner had a second trust deed of $100,000 on the property. While he told me it had been paid off fourteen years earlier, this payoff had never been recorded. The previous escrow company should have—but didn't—recorded a Reconveyance Deed, a document used to show the loan was paid. The next place to check for records would be the old escrow company, but it had closed years ago. When we went to check with the original title company, we learned they had been acquired. When we tried to contact that company, we discovered they were out of business. This was the story with seven different companies.

Naturally, our current title company did not want to insure the title unless we could prove it had been paid. The owner couldn't find the old file or any old monthly bills received from the lender, which would have showed a decreasing balance. The title company did not want to insure it no matter what alternative documents they could find. We tried two more title companies, and they also said no. I prayed for wisdom, knowing God would tell me what to do next.

So, I asked the seller if they could search for any canceled checks. They finally found a check made payable to the bank that held the loan. It was for the amount of their old payment, dated only one month prior to when they said the loan had been paid off. The footnote on the check: "Last payment."

"If we would do a credit report on them, then perhaps this $100,000 loan would show up as paid, and at that date," I thought. Many times old loans that have been paid off will drop off a credit report after ten years. Well, it showed "paid," one month after the check that noted "last payment." The payment amount on the credit report matched the amount on their check. I also had them get all their current checking accounts statements that reflected all their monthly payments. None of them showed any amount being paid for a second trust deed payment. If the second still existed, and they had not been making payments for more than fourteen years, then someone would have filed a notice of default. It would have shown up on the title report, and also it would reflect on their credit report. Of course, there wasn't any. With these three items, and a letter from them stating that it had been paid in full, I felt it would be enough to convince the title company to insure the title, even though they said they would not take any alternative documentation.

We explained this to a manager at the title company, who agreed that it was enough but would still insure around it and list it as an exception. That was good enough for the buyer. The escrow closed after a two-month delay. Feeling led me to pursue this angle; the Lord prompted me to think of those items we needed and gave us favor with the title company. Many times you simply can't take no for an answer. Persistence and being determined will prevail.

FORESIGHT

A friend who was also a real estate broker had been working for a builder at the time the housing market neared a standstill. As the highest-paid employee, she held the highest position—and understood that with everyone else facing layoffs, her time would come. Instead of waiting for her bosses to let her go, she decided to approach them. She told them that they could only afford to pay her one-half of what she had been making.

While they were shocked by her advice to cut her salary in half, Proverbs 27:12 states, "A prudent man foreseeth the evil, and hideth himself; but the simple pass on, and are punished" (KJV).

They respected her honesty, took her advice, and kept her on board. Now, if she hadn't gone to them, they would have let her go, leaving her with no income. Though almost impossible then to find a job, her plan kept her employed. To coin a phrase from the Bible, she saw that the "handwriting was on the wall." (See Daniel 5:5.)

After the economy recovered, guess whom they gave a raise to, and placed her at an even higher position? Would you have recommended your company cut your salary in half? Wisdom is seeing the end result.

CHAPTER 9

THE REALITY OF POVERTY IN OUR WORLD

By Sunday Adelaja

CONSIDER TWO DIFFERENT snapshots.

The first is of a stereotypical suburban family from Kansas City, Missouri, surrounded by all their material belongings. The family of four (two requisite children) stands in front of a luxury home, compared to world standards. Outside are two expensive cars and a brand-new minivan. Scattered around the family home are rooms full of furniture, including an eighty-six-inch-long sofa, king-sized bed, Oriental carpets, various wardrobes, several television sets, radios, telephones, computers, CDs, DVDs, iPods, several bathrooms, modern kitchen equipment, and a library of books. All together, the family owns hundreds of items of every conceivable nature. This depicts the life of a typical suburban family in the United States.

The second snapshot shows a statistically average poor family from a village similar to the Nigerian village of Idomila Ijebu-Ode, Ogun State, where I grew up. All of the family's few earthly possessions are scattered in front of their thatched-roof hut, where the family of ten lives with a goat, a pig, and some chickens. There are few cooking and washing implements. The only food is cassava, a type of yam. There are sticks used for digging and a bundle of wood for firewood, but no electric utensils because there is no electricity in the village. The family owns almost no clothes, besides what each family member is wearing. Their toilet is a hole in the ground outside the hut. All that they own, put together, amounts to maybe a dozen items. This depicts a family with no possessions and little opportunity. It depicts the picture of an earlier century.

On a global scale most people more closely resemble the Nigerian family than the American family. The stark reality is that unlike the typical American family, more than half the people in the world have very little to call their own.

The World Bank defines extreme poverty as living on less than the equivalent of $1.25 per day. Moderate poverty is defined as living on $2.50 a day.[1] By that definition, a man earning $3 per day or $90 per month is not poor. This may seem ludicrous to those living in Western countries. Nevertheless, more than a billion people live on less than a dollar a day, and more than two billion live on less than two dollars per day. In other words, about half the world lives each day on less money than the price of a cup of Starbucks coffee.

As alarming as these facts may be, what's more alarming is that such things could be happening in this twenty-first century. How can a generation that lays claim to such technological breakthrough and innovation allow such disparity to continue unchecked?

Unfortunately, most Americans and others in the Western world are oblivious to the abject poverty and utterly detestable conditions in which the rest of the world lives.

DRIVEN BY NEED OR GREED?

When Westerners are confronted with the blunt facts of global poverty, it becomes immediately apparent that most of the material things they pray for are more driven by *greed* than by *need*.

Greed makes us want more than we can handle. It makes us heap up things until we have to acquire more living space just to keep it all. Greed is the spirit that drives corporate America. It's why corporate downsizing has become so popular while top-level executives earn ridiculously exorbitant bonuses. Greed is pervasive within the Western culture (as well as most of the leadership of the developing world, especially in Africa), and the church is not immune to its vices. We seem to have forgotten that God only promised to meet our needs, not to satiate our greed. The sad reality is that greed is vigorously promoted from the pulpit and by those who are supposed to be society's pillars of truth and justice.

My intention is to sound the alarm and awaken the conscience of people in order to see injustice come to an end. It is not an attempt to judge anyone; rather, it is an attempt to incite awareness in the hopes that we would work to reform our unequal world.

If we have problems using this absolute definition of poverty, we can also look at poverty as a relative idea. That is, we can see poverty as something socially defined, or something that depends on a particular social context. Such a relative measurement would ask us to compare, for example, the total wealth of a segment of the poorest people in the world with the total wealth of a segment of the richest people in the world. These comparisons will be even more bleak and unsettling.

A study several years ago published by a senior World Bank economist showed that the richest fifty million people in Europe and North America have roughly the same income as almost three billion poor people collected from around the world.[2] This 1 percent of the world's population took as large a piece of the pie as the small slice handed to the world's poorest 57 percent of people. Using another illustration, if we use the poverty line as defined by the countries of North America and Western Europe, then the poorest 10 percent of Americans are better off than a full two-thirds of the world's entire population. Early in this century, the World Bank reported that twenty-four developing countries with a population of three billion people were beginning to integrate into the global economy, with a per-capita growth of only 1 percent in the 1960s up to 5 percent in the 1990s.[3] Even so, the state of world economics and the ratios of poverty between the Western world and the developing world are very dramatic. It is no secret that there is inequality among nations. Certain countries of the world have most of the money while others have very little. There is also inequality within nations, for it is a fact that within poor countries there are rich groups of people whose incomes compare to the incomes of wealthy groups in more developed nations. Our sense of goodness and fairness suggests a more equitable distribution of the income of the world. Our sense of fairness and rightness says that within a country, some should not be living in mansions while others scrounge around for food in garbage dumps. It is hard to understand why distribution of wealth is so unequal. Our sense of what is just and appropriate cries out and asks why.

REASONS FOR INEQUALITIES

Why do some countries have so much and others so little? One explanation—this is a result of the market economy. Rich countries are rich because they supply things that are scarce but in high demand. Poor nations are poor because they supply too many things for which there is relatively little demand. This explanation, however, seems somewhat simplistic and does not answer the question of poverty in poor nations such as South Africa, which supplies the world with diamonds,[4] and Nigeria, which is the world's twelfth largest producer and supplier of oil,[5] both commodities that are very much in demand.

Whatever the answer might be, it is clear that inequalities in the world cry out for some form of remedy. During his second term, US president George W. Bush said at a meeting of the Inter-American Development Bank: "A world where some live in comfort and plenty, while half of the human race lives on less than two dollars a day, is neither just nor stable."[6]

This great, magnificent nation that is so technically oriented has created an Achilles's heel—electricity. With one $100,000 missile fired from a used submarine two hundred miles offshore and a few pounds of enriched plutonium exploding over the United States, every form of electricity would stop instantly and for months. In one second we would be living in the nineteenth century.

Where is the world headed?

What is in the immediate future?

If Iran is not stopped in its quest for nuclear weapons, the Iranians will have them soon—and they will use them against Israel. If Iran is stopped, it will happen through military force. Only America and Israel have that power, because Russia is now helping Iran to develop their nuclear weapons. I believe this military action will lead to Russia bringing together a coalition of Islamic nations to invade Israel.

—JOHN HAGEE, *Earth's Final Moments*

One way the world attempts to come to grips with poverty on an international scale is through the concept of foreign aid. This is where poor nations receive money to encourage their growth and economic development. Reasonably rich nations donate money to alleviate poverty in poorer nations. This is especially true when richer countries tout their moral responsibility by pointing to the size of their foreign aid budget. Despite the fact that there seems to be no objective evidence to prove foreign aid stimulates economic development in poor countries, the rich nations continue pledging more money in aid to the world's less-developed nations.

The reality of poverty is that one-third of deaths, some eighteen million people each year (fifty thousand per day), stem from poverty-related causes.[7] That is more than four hundred fifty million people since 1990, the majority women and children, that's more than the population of the United States. Every year more than six million children die before their fifth birthday.[8] These are horrible, sobering facts. Can the Christian church do anything to solve the problem of worldwide poverty and the inequality of wealth distribution? Aside from foreign aid and the economic theories of supply and demand, is there a spiritual dimension to poverty? We must go beyond the economic sphere to blend the laws of economics and spirituality and to address the individual hearts of men and woman as they submit to God in their quest to overcome poverty.

While I am not attempting a study of world poverty or economics, I think we should ask, "Are Christians and the Christian church relevant to the eradication of poverty in the world?" I wish to address Christians, who have access to biblical solutions to this problem, and I want to tell you my thesis right up front: *Christians around the world must become kingdom minded in order for us to help resolve the problem of poverty in our world.* The purpose of the church is not to have people come in and sit down. Rather, it is to go out and change cultures by establishing God's value system. Moreover, this includes God's value system regarding money and wealth. Poverty is not God's will for anyone, and it is outside kingdom purposes for Christians to be struggling in the area of finances, whether personal or societal.

Being kingdom minded is what the apostle Paul calls being "transformed by the renewing of your mind" (Rom. 12:2, KJV). In other books I have addressed applying the principles of the kingdom to the church. Now I want to apply those same principles to individual Christians on questions of money, wealth, and personal finances. Remember, God's kingdom principles apply to money as much as anything else. World poverty is agonizingly real. It will never improve until individual Christians affect the culture of life, change the culture of nations, and improve their own financial situations. Thus, the economic growth of the world must be the priority of individuals in obedience to the teaching of Scripture and the principles of the kingdom of God.

Hence, the reason why a Christian desires financial freedom is not just to meet his or her needs but also to become an answer to the challenges of our world.

The Great Commission of Matthew 28:19–20 is not only about rescuing souls and planting churches; it is about much more. The Great Commission tells us to make disciples of all *nations*. Nations are cultures, and cultures are to be transformed and redeemed by Christ's church taking dominion over God's entire creation on Earth. The purpose of the Great Commission is to change cultures, and this means the church needs a new model or style of missions. God is not satisfied with our church-minded approach. He created everything, and He wants His principles to rule everywhere. That is our assignment in the Great Commission—to permeate the world with the nature and principles of God and to be the Lord's representative in our spheres of influence. If we are in a place, then God is there!

Only the redeemed can improve our world. That is why God is calling Christians all over the world to take up the challenge of conquering the mountain of finances to subdue the earth for God.

THE GOSPEL OF PROSPERITY

I am not writing about the American dream or the well-being of any individual. I am not out to discuss getting money for personal gain, nor about the so-called prosperity gospel. When it comes to teaching financial prosperity, there are many wolves in sheep's clothing. Of course God prospers people, and I believe this as strongly as anyone does. Nevertheless, there is a good deal of error in most American prosperity preaching, as in most countries where the prosperity gospel is preached. It is important to address this matter so that there will be no mistaking this message for the teachings of the prosperity gospel.

THE MAIN ERRORS OF THE PROSPERITY MOVEMENT

The prosperity gospel teaches that one prospers only when giving. Giving is the main emphasis. This is false. True prosperity comes not just when we give, but also when we know the laws of money and discipline ourselves to abide by them. This is the difference between being rich or poor. Although there is an important place for the law of giving, it is only one of many laws. By itself, it will fail to make anyone sustainably wealthy. There is a very sympathetic story of a couple sent by their denomination as missionaries to a different part of Ukraine. Their situation was so bad that they didn't even have money for a bed or a mattress. They and their young child ended up *sleeping on the floor*! In Africa and other third-world countries, this is quite common, but for it to happen in the center of Europe is out of the ordinary.

Though commissioned to go out and save people, they didn't even have the bare minimum for basic living. This young couple was so desperate that they were about to leave the ministry when they came across my teachings on financial freedom.

Subsequently they listened to these teachings and applied the principles to their lives. As a result, several years later, even though they were still full-time pastors, they made their first million US dollars. As a matter of fact, things had gotten so bad for them that they didn't have any starting capital. The young pastor had to borrow one hundred fifty dollars from his father's pension for their first investment.

What is most painful about this story is that prior to this, the couple had been serving in their charismatic denomination for fifteen years. They learned that all they needed for financial prosperity was to be a good Christian, active in ministry, faithful in giving tithes and offerings, and giving additionally to other church projects.

They did this faithfully for fifteen years and even dedicated their lives to missions service—yet the money never came! As they continued to abide by the teachings of the church, they became more impoverished. This is because they were not following the whole truth of kingdom prosperity—only half the truth. Half-truth, however, cannot get the job done. Half-truth is as dangerous as a lack of truth. One aspect of the truth will not make you financially independent. Giving only is not enough to bring you to substantial wealth.

This man has since traveled all over Ukraine and Europe, teaching about these real principles and how ignorance caused him to live a miserable life in poverty, and conversely, how the truth has set him free for financial abundance to minister freely!

In most cases when Christians teach that the only way to be prosperous is by giving to the church or ministry, the only person who becomes wealthy is the one on the receiving end, or those who have control of the collection. Usually this is the pastor, televangelist, or radio preacher, along with his or her inner circle. This leads to a situation where many pastors, especially those of most megachurches, live in the lap of luxury and excess while large portions of their flock can barely afford three square meals a day. It is important that you understand I am addressing the issue of *imbalance*.

Now, many megachurch pastors are quite talented and hardworking. Many have been able to create their own wealth from their book sales and other private enterprises. There is nothing fundamentally wrong with being prosperous and living well from one's exploits. However, there is something fundamentally wrong with exploiting the weak and the innocent for personal gain. There is something wholly unsettling about a Christian leader whose taste for the good life exceeds his sense of justice. This imbalance is not in harmony with the teachings of Jesus Christ.

My focus is to help my readers attain financial freedom. The focus is on *your* well-being, not just that of some preachers. For that, I want to introduce what I believe to be a more biblical model for prosperity. Unlike the corporate model used by most churches where wealth is only accessible to a few at the top of the pyramid, this model is a kingdom model, which empowers all. This model produced more than two hundred millionaires in just two years in the church that I lead. The majority of these people started with nothing. Many were in debt when they started their journey to wealth. All glory belongs to God for giving us the wisdom and insight and for vindicating His Word.

For the preachers of prosperity, financial prosperity is much more than a blessing—it is the right of every believer who claims it. In fact, God wills wealth and riches to all His children. The prosperity movement presents an erroneous view on the gospel of prosperity by limiting wealth creation to the power of confession. You often hear proponents teach that what you say is what you get, or "confessing it means possessing it." Start speaking about it and it will come into being as God creates what you are speaking. This is the *Wheel of Fortune* approach to faith, and it amounts to extortion because it purports to teach people how to make God work at their behest.

Most teachers of prosperity teach an incomplete aspect of financial empowerment. They emphasize faith and belief and never teach about the production of goods and services, and often because they are not comfortable with having to release their controlling grip on the congregation. They never tell their people that true prosperity comes by getting involved in the process of production because they themselves do not understand it. They emphasize faith, belief, and sowing a financial seed, and never teach about the production of goods and services.

John the Revelator described an incredible marching army of two hundred million soldiers from the Orient, marching down the dried-up riverbed of the Euphrates toward Israel. Why would China make this move? China is also thirsty for Arab oil.

When the United States went to war with Iraq in 2003, China began to make a huge shift in its oil policies. Until then most of China's oil had come from Iraq. But with the entry of America into the country of Iraq, China could no longer put all its "oil apples" in the one basket of Iraq's oil reserves. "Iraq changed the government's thinking," said Pan Rui, an international relations expert at Fudan University in Shanghai.[9]

The two kings that remain on the earth at this point in prophecy are the king of the West, which is being led by the Antichrist, and the king of the East, which is China. These two kings and their armies will meet to battle it out for world supremacy on a battlefield in Israel called *Armageddon.*

—JOHN HAGEE, *Earth's Final Moments*

Amazingly, the Donald Trumps of this world profess no faith at all, and yet they sit on top of the pile in the world of finances. It is high time we learned the importance of producing goods and rendering services as a prerequisite to being wealthy. It is not enough just to bring money to the church or pastor; if we do not produce goods and services, we are deceiving ourselves if we expect to gain or sustain wealth. Because of this kind of teaching, even in rich Western societies such as the United States, you often find most people living in the clutch of persistent need instead of living in the abundance they profess. This always shocks me when I travel through the United States.

There is another problem with the prosperity movement: it tends to put the emphasis on the needs of the person. Unfortunately this has produced more self-centered Christians and "what's-in-it-for-me?" Christians. It talks about paying bills and meeting the needs and desires of life (such as cars and houses). I believe, however, that the main purpose of money is not to meet needs, but first to accomplish God's purposes on the earth. Of course, the Lord meets personal needs, but that is not the main reason to desire wealth. God wants us to be rich so we can carry out His purposes. He is more interested in making us channels of blessing to others rather than islands of blessing to ourselves.

POPULAR SCRIPTURES BUT FALSE INTERPRETATIONS

"The wealth of the wicked is laid up for the righteous" is a major doctrine in prosperity-preaching circles. The emphasis is on the fact that God wants to take wealth from the sinner and give it to believers. Proverbs 13:22 does say, "A good man leaves an inheritance to his children's children, but the wealth of the sinner is stored up for the righteous" (NKJV). This is true, and the Bible does not lie. Nevertheless, when preached this way, there is contradiction in the very principles of God's nature. The principles of the justice of God would not allow collecting the wealth of the wicked to give to the Christian, because the Bible teaches in Proverbs 10:4 that the diligent worker will prosper, no matter whether that worker is a believer or not. God makes people rich because of diligence and hard work, not because they are followers of a particular prosperity teacher. There is yet a more tragic consequence of this direction of thinking; it warps the underlying sense of love, kindness, and fairness of its subscribers. Whereas the Bible teaches us to love our enemies, this kind of teaching ends up causing us to hope and pray for the downfall or misfortune of wealthy unbelievers, so we can dispossess them of their wealth.

The way to look at the meaning of Proverbs 13:22 is that we reach wealth when the righteous produce a better product than anyone else on the market. This is because the righteous will produce goods and services not only to impress people but also to please God. The transfer of wealth that prosperity teachers should emphasize is not God taking from the wicked to give to the believer, but rather people buying from the righteous in exchange for the best quality of goods on the market.

Remember, there is no transfer of wealth without Luke 16:10–12: "Whoever can be trusted with very little can also be trusted with much, and whoever is dishonest with very little will also be dishonest with much. So if you have not been trustworthy in handling worldly wealth, who will trust you with true riches? And if you have not been trustworthy with someone else's property, who will give you property of your own?" (NIV). The point here is that the wealth of the world comes only to the believer who produces better goods or services than others in the market. Because most people buy from him, he exchanges his goods for the wealth of the world and the wicked.

"The wicked covet the plunder of evil men, but the root of the righteous yields fruit" (Prov. 12:12, MEV). In this scripture the Bible tells us that only the wicked desires the plunder of other men, even if the man with the plunder is an evil man. It is still wickedness to desire what you did not work for. It is even more alarming that this kind of teaching is coming from a pulpit of a church, because the church is supposed to be a pillar and foundation of truth.

On the other hand, the second half of this verse says: "But the root of the righteous yields fruit," which goes along to tell us that if we are really righteous we will be productive and do things better than other men. We are supposed to be not just productive but also exemplify excellence and perfection in our work. When we do this in the goods we produce and the services we offer, others who wish to flourish will come to us. That is what I mean when I say that the wealth of the wicked will only come to the righteous when the righteous do things better than the rest of the world—so much so that everybody is attracted to them to buy their products and deploy their services.

Some prosperity preachers use another passage of the Bible to push their wares: when the children of Israel left Egypt and God told the Egyptians to give their gold and silver to the Israelites. (See Exodus 12.) They use this as an example of God giving the wealth of the world to the believers. This sounds nice—except that the children of Israel had worked very hard for a very long time in slavery. For centuries Pharaoh did not pay the Jews for their forced labor. After working for so long without compensation, God proved that He is a God of justice. He would not allow the Israelites to leave Egypt without being compensated for their years of hard labor. Technically this was a transfer of wealth on a very large scale, but as you can see, God did not violate His own principles of justice in order to make His children rich and happy.

My basic premise is that prosperity must have as its top priority the advancement of God's kingdom and His righteousness (Matt. 6:33). Christians can build this kingdom by understanding the concept of wealth and touching the whole fabric of society through the creation of wealth. When properly allocated, wealth can become the solution to many of society's problems. Not only can Christians experience financial freedom, but that freedom also affords them the ability to be committed to radical kingdom service.

HOW THE SYSTEM WORKS

There is a popular belief that all people are equal and that everyone has an equal opportunity to make money. This is a cover-up. Even though God makes us equal, manufactured systems work to the advantage of some and to the disadvantage of others. Only a select group of about 5 percent of the world's population has solid and correct information on how to get rich. In addition, you can be sure they have the system constructed in such a way that all things work together for their good and that no one breaks the order.

Outside this cadre of wealthy leaders active in promoting their own self-interests, the rest of the whole world suffers because people do not know the truth about the spiritual dimension of money and riches. The truth is there is more than enough money in the world, and anyone can have a share of this wealth. Because of a lack of knowledge, however, the vast majority of us do not have access to it. I consider this an unfortunate situation, and the time has come to apply the remedy of knowledge and information. Unbalanced prosperity teaching has failed to deliver on its many promises. Within the church it has created a structure similar to that of the world where only those at the top attain wealth. That is why I so strongly resent it. Rather than reducing the scourge of poverty, it has only made it worse by failing to apply the whole counsel of God to the problem.

PRACTICAL WISDOM FOR ASPIRING MILLIONAIRES

1. Successful people know that success is not a gamble or a matter of chance.

2. Successful people know that all success comes by hard work.

3. Real success is a lifetime of learning.

4. Successful people have conditioned themselves to learn from others and from their failures and successes.

5. Successful people learn by practicing what they know on a daily basis.

6. Successful people know that true education is what you get for yourself and by yourself. It is not what someone gives or tells you.

7. Successful people know that true success in life does not come by luck. A lucky man is not a successful man.

8. True winners know that they must develop skills and acquire knowledge before becoming truly successful.

9. A successful man is one who has the knowledge, skills, and expertise that brought him to success.

10. Work your way to success, and don't expect it to come by accident.

KINGDOM PRINCIPLES

1. Over a billion people live on less than a dollar a day, and more than two billion live on less than two dollars per day.[10]

2. The richest fifty million people in Europe and North America have roughly the same income as almost the three billion poor people collected from around the world.[11]

3. The poorest 10 percent of Americans are better off than a full two-thirds of the world's entire population.

4. The reality of poverty is that one-third of deaths, some eighteen million people each year (fifty thousand per day), are due to poverty-related causes.[12]

5. Christians around the world must change cultures by establishing God's value system.

6. World poverty is agonizingly real. It will never improve until individual Christians affect the culture of life, change the culture of nations, and improve their own financial situations.

7. The reason why a Christian desires financial freedom is not just to meet his or her needs, but also to answer the challenges of our world.

8. God is calling Christians all over the world to take up the challenge of conquering the mountain of finances to subdue the earth for God.

9. When Christians teach that the only way to be prosperous is by giving to the church or ministry, the only person who becomes wealthy is certainly not the giver but rather the person or group at the helm of the ministry.

10. The main purpose of money is not to meet needs but first to accomplish God's purposes on the earth.

CHAPTER 10

FINANCIAL FREEDOM AND THE BASIC LAWS OF MONEY

By Sunday Adelaja

As God's children, our goal should always be to be financially free and to depend on our maker alone. Accordingly, nothing should control our lives but Him. To live like this requires that we first conquer the love of money and rise above its controlling power. "A feast is made for laughter, wine makes life merry, and money is the answer for everything" (Eccles. 10:19, NIV). Yes, feasts are for fun, but money is required for them. No money; no party. The simple and indisputable fact is that we need money. We need it to make a feast for God, for our families, and for our generation. The Lord tells us in Psalm 23 that He will prepare a table for us in full sight of our enemies. Notice that even God wants to prepare a table for us. He needs something to work with from our end, which is why we must apply ourselves to work.

Money is responsible for fun. There are two ways to be financially free—either we have no financial responsibilities, making us independent of the influence of money; or we have a surplus supply that frees us from the worry of responsibilities. The first scenario would only apply to a small segment of society, such as children or homeless people. Therefore, the only reasonable way to be finally free would be to have money in abundance. The fact is, we derive satisfaction from things other than parties, nice clothes, comfortable shoes, good cars, and so on. These things are as much a source of satisfaction as they are the source of monetary responsibilities. Still, if you were to try living without them for a year, I seriously doubt whether you would have much fun. Without funds, there is nothing to eat, no gas for our cars, and no clothes to wear.

What did Solomon mean when he said, "Money is the answer for everything"? This means it brings answers or solutions to all questions of life. Everywhere I go, I hear people complain about the lack of money. There is not enough money in Germany, England, Africa, the United States, or Ukraine. Remember, 95 percent of the money in the world is concentrated in the hands of only 5 percent of the world's population. The other 95 percent struggle to grab a part of the remaining 5 percent. Those in possession of the money are the ones who know the principles of wealth creation.

Here we have two major contrasts in financial profiles. As many as 95 percent of the world's people have a shortage of money, and the other 5 percent have abundance. The first group consists of people trying to solve the problem of not having enough money. So they toil from morning until night and end being slaves to money. The latter group of 5 percent has their needs and their children's needs covered. Thus, their only challenges are how to steward their money so that it keeps on turning over interest, and carefully plan to avoid taxes. This is another perk the wealthy 5 percent enjoy—many do not pay much in the way of taxes. What a contrast! Those who can least afford it shoulder the nation's burden of paying taxes, while those who could easily afford it get off scot-free! It is little wonder the rich get richer while the poor are forever getting poorer.

THE LOVE OF MONEY

It is not money itself but rather the love of money that is the root of all evil. When people love money, they are not free from it. People whose thirst for money drives them to that extreme commit a vast majority of the crimes committed in society. As strange as this is, it is not the people with credible wealth but people who do not have money who are usually the ones most affected by the spirit of mammon. Having an excess of wealth creates its own problems, and it has ruined many people. However, a lack of money and the desire to have it is responsible for most crimes and violence.

Just a cursory glance at history will reveal the extent to which this is true in America. Crime flourished during the Great Depression at an alarming rate, even by today's standards. From the street gangs to the more sophisticated crime rings, there were myriads of activities among them, all aimed at making money. During the onset of the recession in 2008, bank robberies increased across America,[1] reaching nearly six thousand for the year.[2] Although declining over the next three years, the FBI says they still totaled nearly forty-five hundred during 2011.[3]

However, the love of money is seen not only in the multiplicity of crimes being committed by the poor, but also in legal activities at the institutional level. In the forty years following *Roe v. Wade*, the 1973 US Supreme Court ruling that legalized abortion, more than fifty-six million babies were legally aborted in America.[4] Some see no wrong in this, while others consider it morally reprehensible. Whichever end of the spectrum you stand on, abortion is a multibillion-dollar federally funded business that continues to flourish under government protection. Pro-life forces in America have fought long and hard to overturn these laws to enhance protection of the unborn, but to little avail. Why the killing of the innocent unborn is allowed to continue can only be explained by the love of money. The same can be said of the pornography industry, which enjoys protection under the First Amendment.

It does not take a genius to see the negative influence of

abortion and pornography. If space permitted, we could also talk about the greed of Wall Street speculators and the effect they have on the price of various commodities and, consequently, the global economy. The love of money affects people from every segment of society. It impacts the rich, the poor, and our institutions.

The point of all this is that you are either the master over money, or you are its slave. Either you make money serve you, or you will end up serving it. Most people believe they are free from the love of money. You can test yourself by asking, "What am I working for?" If it turns out you are working for money alone, then you might be its slave. Christians should not work just for money. Instead, every Christian should go to work with one goal and one purpose in mind—to bring the kingdom of God into the sphere where he or she works. We are His ambassadors in the marketplace. If we are working at a job only because we must survive, then the potential exists for money to control our actions and rule over us.

Working in "survival mode" makes us resort to all manner of desperate acts. Kingdom dwellers must never be motivated by survival but by God's purpose. Jesus went to the cross because He was not concerned about His longevity. He had a single purpose in mind and would not be deterred by threats or criticism. For Jesus, survival was never an issue. He lived and died for the will of the Father. That was His purpose. Therefore, the first purpose of employment should be to bring God's kingdom to rule in our workplace. God gives us plans for making His name known and getting His will done. Paychecks and promotions are just God's way of rewarding our faithfulness in seeking His kingdom first.

America as a whole wants short, high-tech military campaigns with shock and awe that end in Washington, DC, with massive parades down Pennsylvania Avenue on national television, such as we had in Desert Storm. Long, drawn-out wars of attrition, as in Vietnam, will be part of our past—not our future. When America sees Russia and the Arabs going into Israel, it will be simply a war above and beyond its national will to respond. Russia and the Arab nations will form one of the most impressive military forces ever put together. As Ezekiel says, "It will cover the land." Ezekiel makes it clear that America's and Europe's diplomatic inquiry means absolutely nothing to Russia and the Arabs. The invasion is on!

—JOHN HAGEE, *Earth's Final Moments*

For me, work is service to God, a way of establishing the kingdom of heaven on Earth. Of course, I want to have a decent salary, but a decent salary is not my primary goal. Instead, I want to be an example to my coworkers that God will provide everything necessary in life. If you are motivated by something different than that, you need to change. All work should be service to God; money is only a by-product of such services.

WHO IS YOUR GOD?

The tragedy of the twenty-first century is that people—especially in the West—serve money instead of making money serve them. It is sad to see how so many have become slaves to money. It is true the Lord wants us to prosper, but there is a purpose for prosperity. It is ultimately for the prosperity of God's kingdom in this world. While acquiring riches, avoid stepping away from the boundaries of that goal. If you devote yourself to this purpose, uprooting all selfish ambitions and egoism from your heart, then the Lord—who looks at the heart—will sanctify you and make you a channel for His glory.

When you devote yourself to the promotion of God's kingdom, you can prepare for blessings. God does not give money so much as He *entrusts it* to those who are pure in heart. He can only trust those who are dedicated to working tirelessly to establish His rule. These are the principles that move us toward wealth before we actually receive financial blessings. They must be deeply entrenched in our hearts. Would you like God to entrust you with millions? If your answer is yes, what will you do if someone actually gives you five million dollars? During one of the numerous seminars I conduct in our church, I asked these two questions. Here are some responses from people who thought they were ready to be millionaires:

1. *I would fast, pray, and ask God what He would want me to do with the money.*

   This is no answer at all, because if we do not already know what we need money for, then we really do not need it. Money comes only in response to vision, because when there is vision, money moves in its direction. Vision leads to provision.

2. *I have a few ideas. I would buy a piece of property and build a rehab center. I would buy buildings for other ministries and help them financially.*

   This sounds worthwhile, even spiritual, but spending money that way only leads to spending *all* the money reserved. Soon that person will be penniless again. Before spending money on charities, multiply it first.

3. *I would invest the money in arts and media for the Word of God to be preached on television and in theaters.*

   This answer is similar to the previous one in that this mind-set only devours the finances instead of generating a source by which it would constantly generate more funds for future use.

4. *I would build houses for homeless people. I would also give money to students who can't pay for their education.*

   A wrong understanding of money makes people

assume that their first duty to money is to spend it. On the contrary, the first law of money says do not spend it; instead, invest it.

5. *I would invest the money and make a profit. Then, I would buy a building for the church.*

This answer is much better. The responses I received in my own congregation show that only one out of five Christians understands what to do with money. Wise people know they only spend the proceeds from one's capital, but never the basic capital.

These answers point to the fact that most people are not prepared enough for God to entrust us with money. He also knows how each one of us would really use the money. One thing is certain—God will never entrust wealth to someone not ready to handle it. He is our Creator, and He knows us better than anyone else does. He also knows whether we would have enough wisdom to make the right choices. For most of us, a single day would probably be enough to dispose of the money and be left with nothing. This is the problem of not knowing and abiding by the laws of money.

THE PARABLE OF THE TALENTS

In the twenty-fifth chapter of the Gospel of Matthew, Jesus told the parable about the talents and thereby explained the laws of money. The servant hoarding the talent and not investing it was punished and rebuked for his wickedness. The other two servants received three and five talents of money. They invested and multiplied it, and their rewards were handsome. If we are going to invest money, we need to know how to do it and what to invest in. Many people go bankrupt because they sow good seed into bad soil, and that is the surest way to lose one's hard-earned money.

It is obvious that the last servant did not have an appreciation of the value of the talent committed to his trust and had not learned enough to know how to invest properly in moneymaking ventures. Preparation for riches implies rich saturation on the inside with God and His kingdom principles. Usually, riches do not come suddenly. The reason is that God uses a systematic approach to entrust us with money and wealth.

At first, He may give us one thousand or five thousand dollars just to test our wisdom in its use. However, maybe He has a million dollars in mind for us. What we do with the one thousand or five thousand dollars will determine whether we will get the rest of the money God is keeping for us. So even though God intends for all His children to live in abundance, only a few will because most do not possess the knowledge necessary to bring the millions to them.

Churches receive tithes and offerings every week, but most of them run their budgets to the limit way before the month is over. This problem reflects ignorance of what the Bible teaches. In the parable of the talents the servants who received five and two talents multiplied them for their master. On the other hand, the servant with one talent chose not to invest it, which earned a stiff rebuke and stern punishment. Why are we surprised that there are few millionaires in our churches? There will never be many people with significant money to benefit the church as long as we do not understand the concept of money. Stewardship is demanded from each one of us, including nations, nongovernmental organizations (NGOs), and even churches. If a church is not a good steward of the tithes and offerings of the people, God cannot trust that church with more money. God expects us to multiply some of the money and keep it for the future to carry out His will on the earth.

THE BASIC LAWS OF MONEY

The first law of money is *multiplication*. The two faithful servants did not *spend* the money given them, but rather *multiplied* it. Even the third servant did not spend his money, but stored it up. Yet this man was condemned. I have advised the pastors of our daughter churches to take 30 percent from the monthly tithes and offerings and put it aside for savings and investments. I tell them to turn this money into a harvest. In other words, put it aside for multiplication and not spend everything right away on rent and other needs. If 30 percent is too much, I tell them to start with 10 percent. If a church would faithfully steward God's resources this way, then that church could teach individuals to do the same with their incomes. This is the first law the parable teaches.

The second law of money, which the third servant failed, is *retention*. The servant failed in this because he did not even retain the money entrusted to him. After hiding the money for some time, the initial amount he received had depreciated through inflation. Even though he gave it back to his master upon his return, its inherent value was not intact as this servant so smugly thought. Hence, his master's disappointment. In the same way, we are often tempted to spend all our money on pressing and legitimate needs, but wise people keep some in their possession to invest. Every time God gives us talents, He expects us to multiply them. It is irresponsible to spend money before it multiplies. Churches and individuals tend to find excuses why they cannot invest, but excuses are the comfort of mediocre people. If God trusts you with five talents, multiply them by ten or even thirty before spending them. Moreover, remember that you can only spend the profit from your multiplication of the original talents, not the seed itself, because the seed belongs to God. Spending all of one's salary every month before any of it multiplies is contradictory to the laws of God and human logic. The Lord often does not trust us with money, because we do not understand His ways. We think Jesus was just sharing a nice, quaint parable about money when, actually, He was teaching us how to live. No matter how small your income, keep a part of it for multiplication. The same applies to local churches. If we keep on giving excuses, then we are only encouraging our members to do the same thing—first, to be irresponsible with little, and then to start begging God for a financial breakthrough. What a paradox!

We see the third law of money exemplified in the two faithful servants who were diligent. Diligence means making a meticulous, conscientious, thoughtful, and careful effort in rendering service. It is not just doing something right, but also doing something thoroughly and effectively. Diligence delivers excellence, quality, creativity, and the highest standards possible. (See Proverbs 12:24; 22:29.) Money comes to those who are diligent and who know what to do with it. The servants were faithful because they multiplied their seeds while retaining the original seed and then simultaneously multiplying the seeds again. This third stage is the stage of *investment*.

A revelation from God is a reliable starting capital. Every day the Lord brings drug addicts, prostitutes, and alcoholics to our church in Kyiv for whom we need to care. Who will take care of them, and who will pay for it all? The funds will come from the tithes and offering from the church. How can we multiply these when most people in Ukraine are poor and struggling financially? By diligent saving and investment. Many of my fellow citizens have apartments costing in the neighborhood of $150,000 to $200,000, and yet they do not have money for food. So I asked: "Why not sell the apartment or take a loan on it and buy another one outside the city at a cost two or three times cheaper? Why not invest the rest of the money in real estate and resell it later?" Using this principle, a man in our church became the owner of five apartments instead of one and set out towards making a million.

Money comes to people who know what to do with it; their knowledge is like a magnet that attracts more riches. We need to stop poverty, and, if we are to stop poverty, it must begin in our minds. I want to relate to you the testimony of another one of our church members, who I will call Kate.

> I serve God in the worship team. One day I heard the Lord telling me to take responsibility for the building of the

church. Confused, I thought to myself, "How am I going to do this?" But God simply repeated His request: "Take responsibility and be in accordance with My will. I will send money through you. This is your task, to receive it and apply it according to My purpose." I agreed to be this channel for God. I had been working in real estate for the past nine years, and the whole time I had been practicing the principles of God regarding money.

I both invest and give. God is faithful and has blessed me abundantly. Whenever I had some decent amount of money, I would pray vigorously to find out where the money was supposed to go. By God's grace, I was able to rent an apartment for a minister. Then I found out that a church had a problem keeping up with payments for the rent of their building. I felt the Lord telling me to start paying the rent for them. Since this was such a big responsibility, I asked God for a confirmation. I really wanted to know that the Lord was going to do this thing through me. I had been trying to sell an apartment that was on the real estate market for three years. Therefore, I asked the Lord to help me sell the apartment as a confirmation that whatever I heard was from Him. The next day there were several people vying for the apartment! God told me He is giving billions of dollars to churches and that there will be companies working directly and exclusively for the kingdom and its needs. I believe the time will come that the Lord will bless me so much that I will be able to live on 5 percent from the profit and give the rest.

Notice that Kate gave not just to meet her needs. She first invested to multiply her capital (seed) numerous times over, and only after that she gave from her overflowing profits to meet the needs around her.

Indeed, the Lord is ready to give large amounts of money to Christians dedicated to the kingdom of God. We need to be ready to give as much as God says to give and not just tithes and offerings. We must remember, however, that there are conditions.

One condition is integrity. We need to have God's character, purity, and honesty. We need to be ready to suffer rather than to bring reproach to God's name. If you do not bring God's holiness into your field of work, then you are not ready for true blessings. As I have already stated, God *entrusts* finances and does not *give* them. Can He trust you with wealth, or are you an untrustworthy servant? To be trustworthy, you must be faithful in living by the laws of money first before you could expect to be God's channel of financial blessings.

MY WAKE-UP CALL

I will share my story of how God gave me a wake-up call about how much I had been an unfaithful servant in the area of personal shameful stewardship, as well as in the church's finances. At this time, we were running well over fifteen thousand members, yet never had as much as a million US dollars in our savings account. Our financial life was a constant pocket-to-mouth experience. Whatever we got was what we spent. The paradox here was that when we were only a one-thousand-member congregation, we had exactly the same challenge.

When we had only one thousand members, we were collecting twenty thousand US dollars in offerings monthly. At the end of the month we were always out of money until the following service. In spite of the fact that we had grown to more than fifteen thousand members and were receiving ten times more in offerings, we had the same problem. As our income grew, so did our expenses. I could not solve this puzzle. We prayed, fasted, and expected wealthy converts to bail us out—all to no avail.

Needless to say, that same cycle repeated itself in my personal life and in the lives of most members. This situation continued until a fateful day when God challenged and rebuked me from the Book of Matthew, chapter 25. After I finished preaching to my staff on the lazy and wicked servant who hid his talent, God showed me I was worse than that "wicked, lazy servant" described in verse 26. (Ironically I prided myself on pastoring the nation's largest church.)

After long sessions of meditation, I realized that this parable was actually a lesson on what our attitudes should be toward money—not just talents, as in gifts or callings only. It was a lesson about money management. God made me realize that, if the first law of money was to multiply it and not spend it, I failed this test personally and as a pastor. I also failed in the second law of money, which is retention. I did not retain what I got. I failed worst of all in the third law, which is investment of God's resources. I learned that you should never desire to make money as a minister—if you do, you are greedy and worldly. It does not matter if you are going to use it for God's purposes or not.

Through Matthew 25 God showed me I was not a good steward of His resources. Moreover, Paul and other apostles actually worked apart from preaching, praying, and fasting. They gave a good account of themselves, both as ministers and as merchants in the marketplace.

What shattered my charismatic dogma was when God pointed out to me that the wicked and lazy servant was better than I was because he at least obeyed the law of retention. I, on the other hand, failed all three. At least the wicked servant in the parable understood not to automatically spend his money. Yet I was failing miserably with this law. I imagined where I would have been financially if I had at least kept what God had entrusted into my hands, both on a personal basis and for the church finances. Then I broke down in repentance.

I believe that after years of repeated acts of violent terrorism by Islamic fanatics—such as Madrid, Spain; September 11, 2001, in New York City; and the brutal attack in the London subways of July 7, 2005, killing about fifty people and wounding hundreds— the Western nations have become gun-shy about attacking a Russian-Arab military force.

Whatever the reason, Ezekiel portrays Russia as being in complete command. Why? Because the defender of Israel, the God of Abraham, Isaac, and Jacob, has a hook in Russia's jaw, dragging it into Israel for the greatest object lesson the world has ever seen. There is comfort and consolation in Ezekiel's prophetic portrait of the world tomorrow. The message is that God is in total control of what appears to be a hopeless situation for Israel.

—JOHN HAGEE, *Earth's Final Moments*

However, even as I seemingly repented, I quickly backtracked and tried to justify my actions. I kept telling myself that if I had not spent the money, I could never have covered all the church's expenses and mine. We needed to pay not only our rent and utilities, but also other bills, including those for our many outreaches. The spirit of self-justification was all over me until I finally understood that God was telling me to start with a minimum of 10 percent. That 10 percent would later be invested for multiplication. A ten-time multiplication gives me the total amount collected originally. If I do this every month and invest at least 10 to 20 percent annually, the compound monthly and yearly interest would be enormous.

That is exactly what I started doing. By the end of that year, we already had over a million US dollars in our church's account. I realized that as soon as you apply these financial laws into your business, God begins to open supernatural contacts, relationships, and other doors of unlimited opportunity. This happened to our church and to me. As soon as we started applying the principles, our income grew tremendously. Initially this occurred without members' awareness. However, once they heard of the changes, another miracle took place. Some of the most faithful businesspeople in the congregation saw the sense and wisdom in this approach to church finances. They began offering incredible business and investment opportunities to the church, leading us to gain in returns a minimum of 30 percent annual interest on all our investments. Some offered to multiply our resources at the expense of their time, energy, and giftings.

When I saw how this principle worked for the church, I decided to be a good steward of my personal finances. As I applied these principles in my life, God opened doors, enabling me to make my first million dollars in nine months. It was after this that I decided to study the topic more thoroughly. Then, on a weekly basis for the next two years, I taught these principles of economic and financial empowerment to my church. As a result, we produced over two hundred millionaires in a span of two years.

One of them was a twenty-year-old girl who came to our church with nothing, and in less than two years earned her first million dollars. Then she helped raise up other young people financially who have a heart for God's kingdom. She also decided to live *below* her income status. Even though she was earning ten thousand dollars per month, she refused to buy a car, house, apartment, or any other lavish expenditure. She continued to rent an apartment and use public transportation while contributing 50 percent of her income to various kingdom projects. The rest she continued to invest and multiply, leaving a mere 1 percent to live on—and, in her own words, "To live as a queen."

This story is so unlike many others who live *above* their financial status. Many will even take out a loan so that they can live extravagantly, when in reality they can't afford it at all! Yet she understood that she should not be concerned with public opinion and social expectations. She decided to abide by the laws of money—even after she had earned substantially—and continue to multiply her money before expenditure.

The pattern of all truly wealthy people is to live below their financial means so they can continue with investments and multiplication. Hence, the saying remains true: *the rich get richer as the poor get poorer!*

THE TWENTY BASIC LAWS OF MONEY
THAT I TAUGHT TO MY CONGREGATION

1. God made us to live by laws, not by miracles or mysteries. Money comes to those who know and abide by its principles.

2. Knowledge of the law of money is the key demand for wealth. To obtain this knowledge, find mentors, coaches, teachers, and partners for wealth.

3. After you have given your tithe and offerings to the Lord, the next thing to do with money is save.

4. Income does not determine wealth; knowledge does.

5. Minimize expenses.

6. Don't steal. Pay your tithes and taxes. For a secure future, pay all your debts.

7. Wealth comes by investment. Save in order to multiply the savings, retain by minimizing costs, and multiply by investment and production.

8. Don't listen to the dictates of money—it is a good tool but a bad master.

9. Wealth does not come by working harder, longer, or even wiser. It comes by applying principles, time, energy, your mind, and your money. (See Luke 19:24–26.)

10. It is easier to obtain wealth in poor surroundings than in rich or developed surroundings with already-maximized potential, so never complain about your circumstances.

11. Ignore social expectations demanding a certain standard of social behaviors.

12. Money does not come because someone is good, spiritual, or lucky. It comes to those who know and apply the principles of money. (See Proverbs 6:6–11.)

13. There are no limits in life except those of the mind.

14. Don't keep liabilities. Keep only assets.

15. The reason for failure in life is ignorance and laziness.

16. Do not despise the day of small beginnings. Start with small savings.

17. The windows of heaven are open to send blessings, not money. God sends ideas and designs, but He does not send money. (See Deuteronomy 8:18.)

18. Let God become your partner.

19. Money comes by cultivating your land and producing goods and services.

20. God's blessing is important for enduring wealth without sorrow. God's blessing is the guard against evil.

Each one of these laws took me a month to communicate to my members because the bottom line was not just to give them information; what was even more important was to change their mind-sets. When it comes to money and wealth creation, belief system is the key. It took a lot of breaking and humiliation before God before I changed my own religious concepts to line up with the new revelations that God was giving me. It is possible that you are now in the same position with religious stereotypes and beliefs that prevented God from answering my prayer for financial breakthrough.

Therefore, I would like to challenge every reader to examine yourself, as to your own concept of ministry and finances that you have come to believe because of one dogma or another. I encourage you not to just read through these principles, but also to examine these new points of view. Pray about it and write down in a journal areas where you need to amend your personal and ministry finances.

Earlier in this chapter I listed responses members of my church gave as to how they would spend five million dollars. We saw that most people who were dreaming of becoming millionaires one day had the wrong attitude toward money—they were more sentimental than financially logical.

Because of this, they might be working and struggling through life, dreaming of becoming wealthy one day, but yet fail because their zeal was not according to knowledge.

I can assume that most people might be in that category, and you can decide for yourself which of the five respondents represent your views. We must strive to gain adequate knowledge of money first before striving to gain wealth. Make sure you don't just strive to learn these principles but understand them. Don't just read them, but also study them diligently before you step out to apply what you have learned. The more you know about the principles of money, the better for you in application.

PRACTICAL WISDOM FOR ASPIRING MILLIONAIRES

1. Steadfast millionaires find their joy and contentment in life by pursuing their God-given dreams, not in pursuing material acquisition.

2. They study and work hard to learn more, and then they convert that knowledge into profits.

3. True millionaires invest not just their money, but also their time in getting more knowledge and wisdom. Even their hobbies help them grow financially and personally.

4. True millionaires shun opportunities to get rich quickly and get-rich schemes. They prefer building their wealth in widespread ventures.

5. True millionaires like to understand what they are doing. They focus on building and controlling each step of the way.

6. Legitimate millionaires live below their means and do not concentrate on living big.

7. Faithful millionaires are givers but not wasters of money, both in the family and in the church.

8. True millionaires understand that they are blessed to bless others.

9. They build a future for their children and grand-children, and they support their churches and other Christian ministries.

10. Genuine millionaires are frugal in that they control their expenses and do not waste anything.

KINGDOM PRINCIPLES

1. The only way to be finally free is to have money in abundance.

2. Ninety-five percent of people have a shortage of money, while the other 5 percent have abundance.

3. It is not money itself but rather the love of money that is the root of all evil.

4. Christians should not work for money, but instead, every Christian should go to work with one goal and one purpose in mind: to bring the kingdom of God into the sphere where he or she works.

5. Work is service to God, a way of establishing the kingdom of heaven on Earth.

6. All work should be service to God, and money is only a by-product of such services.

7. Money comes only in response to vision, because when there is vision, money moves in its direction. Vision leads to provision.

8. It is irresponsible to spend money before it multiplies.

9. Money comes to people who know what to do with it; their knowledge is like a magnet that attracts more riches.

10. God made us to live by principles, not by miracles or mysteries.

CHAPTER 11

THE LAND MINE OF FAILING TO PLAN

By James L. Paris

A s of 2012, 70 percent of Americans retire in poverty with few assets, leaving them dependent on family, charities, and Social Security for income.[1] Many people don't make this discovery until they retire and are astonished to find themselves living at or below the poverty line. This should be no surprise. You can take to heart the adage: *Failing to plan is planning to fail.*

Proverbs 6:6–9 says that even lowly ants prepare for the future. Christians have a responsibility to plan ahead. We have many issues with which to deal, such as retirement, our children's education, and funding charitable and religious organizations. God can use us, but only if we have enough foresight to plan.

Most people fail to plan because they are forever waiting at the dock for their ship to come in. "When I get a raise, I will start saving," they say, or "When I get a better job, I will make sure I save some of my income," or "When my student loans are paid off, then I'll start a retirement plan." If this is your strategy, you will probably never start a savings plan. Remember the simple ant, who doesn't make excuses.

Once you have disciplined yourself so that you are not spending more than you earn, you need to take a closer look at what you do with those earnings. As impossible as it may seem now, you can begin to save. In fact, for your own good and that of your children, you *must* save.

GOALS

The basics of a savings plan start with setting goals. What is a goal? Some have called it a dream with a date for achievement. We must look at our circumstances and decide what we want to accomplish in the near future and the extended future.

Once we have decided on our dream, the next step is to place it on a timeline. For example, some people set New Year's resolutions, but most of these resolutions fail because they are not accompanied by a proper plan. A plan starts by setting a goal, establishing a deadline, and then planning strategies to meet that goal within that time frame.

For many years my family vacationed in Florida, which meant a twenty-four-hour drive from Chicago. My father always had a route mapped out, and he could estimate when we would arrive. We never ended up in California or Montana—always in Florida. Why? Because my father had a plan.

Did you know that Americans spend more time planning family vacations than their personal finances? Sad, but true. We need to have a plan for our finances just as we do for other areas of life.

When I have conducted financial seminars, invariably at least one person would approach me and say, "Jim, someday I would like to be rich." When I ask for a definition of rich, the response is usually something like, "I don't know" or "I've never really thought about it."

People with a goal but no plan for reaching it are setting themselves up for disappointment. There is nothing very technical or magical about reaching your financial goals as long as you have a carefully conceived plan.

The components for a financial plan are:

× The desired amount of savings.

× The length of time you have to save.

× The interest rate you expect to earn (an average rate over the life of the plan).

Knowing this information will enable you to arrive at an amount you need to set aside monthly to reach that desired savings.

God continues expressing His love for Israel, saying, "I will bless those who bless you, and I will curse him who curses you" (Gen. 12:3, NKJV). This is and has been God's foreign policy toward the Jewish people from Genesis 12 until this day. Any man or nation that persecutes the Jewish people or the State of Israel will receive the swift judgment of God. Today America finds itself bogged down in an unprovoked, worldwide war with radical Islamic terrorists with no end in sight. America is very vulnerable to terrorist attacks in the future, whose consequences could be much more severe than the three thousand lives lost on 9/11. This is not a time to provoke God and defy Him to pour out His judgment on our nation for being a principal force in the division of the land of Israel.

—JOHN HAGEE, *Earth's Final Moments*

The easiest way to determine the components to achieve your financial goals is to obtain a financial calculator. This is like a regular pocket calculator, except it has some extra keys. It gives you the ability to compute things that would otherwise be complex to figure out. For example, you can determine what the future value will be of your savings today, based on certain interest rates (even with the declines in recent years, you will have more money at the end of five years if you set it aside than if you spend it). The calculator can work out monthly payments that are necessary to meet your financial goals. They are available at numerous outlets or online for less than twenty dollars, although programmable kinds can run between eighty dollars or more.

With a computer, iPad, or other digital device, you can find programs or apps that will perform these functions and much more. Apps allow business owners to perform a variety of valuations, risk-return analysis, and other calculations without having to use a spreadsheet. Some versions are free, although professional upgrades usually carry a charge. The point is: there is no reason for you to remain uninformed about your financial future.

The instructions included with a financial calculator will guide you through its simple operation. These keys will be of greatest value:

- ✕ FV   future value
- ✕ PV   present value
- ✕ I   interest rate
- ✕ PMT   payment
- ✕ N   time

For an example, let's assume a father wants to send his newborn child to a four-year public university in eighteen years. He estimates what the tuition will be in eighteen years, and with the calculator he determines that he must save seventy-five dollars per month in order to have the cash available for that school.

Saving for retirement is no different. Suppose a twenty-five-year-old woman would like to retire at age sixty-five with $1 million. She assumes that she will make an average return of

12 percent on her savings. She will need to save $85 dollars per month for forty years in order to achieve this.

Goals can provide incredible motivation. Knowing that steadily saving that $85 dollars will eventually lead to a million-dollar nest egg can put the spark in some people to make a determined effort to stick to this plan. Goals can take many forms. Perhaps your family wishes to buy a boat. Decide how much that boat will cost and when you would like to buy it. From that data you will be able to determine how much money you will need to save monthly.

If you are planning to purchase an item for which it will take you several years to save, keep in mind that inflation will likely change the price of your purchase. Base your plan on a cost that allows for a reasonable rate of inflation in the cost of that item.

Example: Planning for retirement

Paul and Mary Brown would like to have $500,000 for retirement when Paul is sixty-five. Paul is currently thirty-five. They assume they will be earning 8 percent interest on their investments. What is the monthly savings they need to reach their goal?

- ✗ PV (present value)   =   0
- ✗ FV (future value)   = $500,000
- ✗ N (time)   =   360 months (30 years)
- ✗ I (interest rate)   =   8 percent
- ✗ PMT (payment)   = $335.48

It is very difficult to take any meaningful action on a regular basis without having a goal in mind. Do you think this couple would have the diligence to save $335.48 per month if they had no idea how much it would be worth in thirty years? Probably not.

If Paul and Mary waited until age forty to start this plan, with the same goal of $500,000 at age sixty-five, their monthly savings would need to be almost $200 more. By waiting until Paul is forty-five, the monthly payment will rise to $848 to accomplish the same result. At age fifty the monthly payment is a staggering $1,444!

The reason for these seemingly disproportionate increases is compound interest. The earlier savings have more years to accumulate interest, and these additional funds become part of the investment. The moral: start saving for retirement in your early years, even if the amount is small.

You can see this principle in the work sheet in table 2. First, determine the lump sum of money you will need upon retirement (in today's dollars). Your yearly income will come from the interest returns on this lump sum. For example, you may expect an interest rate of 10 percent, and you would like to have $50,000 a year when you retire. Therefore you need to accumulate a lump sum of fifty thousand times ten, or $500,000. (If you would like to calculate from a more conservative estimate of an 8 percent return, simply use a multiplier of 12 instead of 10.)

Then look at the chart in your work sheet and use your age and your expected rate of return on investing your retirement savings to find your monthly savings cost per thousand.

Example: Buying a car

Mike Keaton wants to pay cash for his next car. He wants to buy this automobile four years from today, when he estimates it will cost $20,000. Mike assumes that he can make 12 percent on his investment. How much will Mike need to save per month?

✗	PV	=	0
✗	FV	=	$20,000
✗	N	=	48 months
✗	I	=	12 percent
✗	PMT	=	$326 per month

If Mike knows he doesn't have $326 a month to stash away, he needs to refigure. Either he should settle for a less expensive car, or try to save for a longer period. He could assume a higher rate of return on his investment, but that would be rolling the dice.

Example: Saving for college

Anita and Bill Thompson have a five-year-old daughter, Amanda. They wish to send her to college at age eighteen. They plan to have $50,000 for this purpose. Bill feels that 10 percent is a reasonable rate of return. How much should they set aside?

✗ PV   =   0

✗ FV   = $50,000

✗ N   =   156 months (13 years)

✗ I   =   10 percent

✗ PMT   = $157 per month

Even with low inflation in recent years, college costs are steadily rising at rates above inflation. Bill and Anita should watch college costs and inflation closely in case they need to adjust their goal and, consequently, their savings.

Example: Mired in debt

While actual rates are much lower today, I am using these examples to give you an idea of the kind of problem excessive debt can cause. For example, although near the end of 2014 thirty-year mortgage and car loan rates were both around 4 percent, the average credit card still charged 15 percent. So take advantage of those ever-present "consolidation" credit cards or line-of-credit offers you find in the mail or online and you could be facing a scenario similar to Tina's.

Tina Reynolds bought a car last year and also got a little loose with her credit cards at Christmas. Now she owes $20,000 in consumer debt. The average of all the interest rates she is currently paying is 15 percent. She wants to be out of debt in two years. How much will she need to pay each month to reach her goal?

- ✗ PV   = $20,000
- ✗ FV   =   0
- ✗ N   =   24 months
- ✗ I   =   15
- ✗ PMT   = $969 per month

Tina should pay off the credit cards with the highest interest rates first in order to bring down the high cost of the interest she is paying. And, of course, cutting up those cards so as not to incur more debt is essential!

When I went to West Berlin in 1984 as a guest of the U.S. military to speak in their annual week of spiritual renewal, I was taken by a German tour guide through Checkpoint Charlie into East Berlin. What a contrast between capitalism and Communism....Separating East and West Germany were two ten-foot-high barbed-wire fences with a no-man's-land of one hundred yards filled with machine gun towers and German shepherd attack dogs. The German tour guide turned to me and fired a question I did not see coming: "Pastor Hagee, why did God allow the Russians to build fences around the German people, with machine guns and attack dogs?"

The answer flashed out of my mouth like lightning: "God allowed the Russians to build barbed-wire fences around the German people to hold you as prisoners with machine guns and German shepherd attack dogs because the German people did exactly the same thing to the Jews at every death camp. You did this at Dachau and Auschwitz, and for every Jew who died, you will have to answer to God."

—JOHN HAGEE, *Earth's Final Moments*

Example: Paying off mortgage early

Mike and Connie Hall have a thirty-year mortgage at 8 percent fixed interest. They are interested in prepaying the principal balance in order to own the house free and clear in ten years. The mortgage amount is $100,000; and their current payment is $733 per month.

What should they be paying in order to retire the mortgage in ten years?

✗ PV	=	$100,000
✗ FV	=	0
✗ N	=	120 months
✗ I	=	8
✗ PMT	=	$1,213 per month (additional principal payments of $480)

As I mentioned, the interest rates in these examples are simply for illustration. You should be aware of the current trends in interest rates in order to make sound estimates for your planning.

SUMMARY

Setting goals is critical to financial success. In order to reach these goals, you must first quantify them. How much? How soon? What are your dreams? How much would you like to have set aside for retirement? Put your goals in writing, with careful attention to the specifics.

Secondly, the goals must be accompanied by a plan that

includes a time frame. Having no plan for your financial future means that you are allowing precious months and years to slip away. This is the most dangerous land mine of all because it is a slow killer; it cannot be reversed. Time can be your greatest ally or your greatest enemy. Once you realize that you have neglected to plan, it may be too late.

Stick with the plan. Set aside those payments. Monitor the plan every six months by checking the rate of inflation and the interest rates that you are earning to decide if you need to modify your plan.

Even if you have to start out on a small scale, such as saving $10 each month, the important thing is that you have grasped the concept and have caught the vision to plan for the future. Getting started is the first hurdle; continuing to save is essential to the result.

Are financial goals a priority in your life? Are they important enough to warrant some of your attention? I think they are, and I urge you to spend time developing those goals and the plans to make them work.

Planning is essential regardless of your circumstances. For example, one person who heard a presentation raised the question of what to do when you are self-employed. He commented, "Because I am self-employed, I'm not quite sure what amount of money I am going to make from month to month. It varies so much that it's difficult for me to follow the principles you teach about setting up a plan."

Such a scenario is becoming increasingly common in an era of corporate downsizing, the virtual office, 24/7 smart phones, and remote access—literally from anywhere in the world. As more people work from home, or start their own businesses, fluctuating income is more likely for millions. Whether you are a self-employed entrepreneur or a sales rep whose income is tied to constantly-changing market forces and interest rates, you need to determine your average earnings.

Let's say in a six-month period your income is $4,000 the first month, $4,000 the second month, $0 the third month, $12,000 the fourth month, $0 the fifth month and $4,000 in the sixth month. Your total income is $24,000, or $4,000 per month. So base your budget and your investment plan on a $4,000 per month average income, setting aside reserves in the months when you meet or exceed the average. The temptation is to spend everything you make each month, but this is dangerous because you are not compensating for the months when you earn nothing.

Use the work sheets on the following pages to help establish your plans.

MONTHLY BUDGET WORK SHEET

Month of _____, _____

Monthly Income:

Salaries _____

Other _____

Total Income _____

Monthly Expenses:

Savings _____

Food _____

Rent/mortgage _____

Electricity _____

Telephone _____

Other utilities _____

Household expenses _____

Auto expense _____

Insurance _____

Loans _____

Education _____

Clothing _____

Laundry, cleaning _____

Personal care _____

Entertainment _____

Gifts _____

Miscellaneous _____

Tax-Deductible Expenses:

Withholding taxes _____

Medical expenses _____

Contributions _____

Home loan interest _____

Child care _____

Miscellaneous _____

Total Expenses _____

TABLE 2
RETIREMENT FUNDING WORK SHEET
HOW TO DECIDE ON A MONTHLY SAVINGS PLAN FOR RETIREMENT

Your Age Now in Years	Monthly Savings Cost Per Thousand (B) at 10% Rate of Return*	Monthly Savings Cost Per Thousand (B) at 12% Rate of Return*	Amount Needed to Equal 1,000 Dollars at Time of Retirement (4% Inflation Assumed)
25	$ .78	$ .42	$4,939
30	1.07	.63	4,045
35	1.47	.95	3,313
40	2.04	1.44	2,713
45	2.93	2.25	2,222
50	4.39	3.64	1,820
55	7.27	6.48	1,490
60	15.78	14.96	1,222

1) Estimate the lump sum needed at retirement, using today's dollars. _____ (dollars needed per year) x 10 = _____ (A)

2) Referring to the above chart as to your age, determine your monthly savings cost per thousand and the expected rate of return for the money you are saving toward retirement.

_____ (B)

3) Use the following formula to determine monthly savings needed:

_____ (A) ÷ 1,000 = _____ (C)
_____ © x _____ (B) = _____
(monthly savings needed)

Example: You are forty years old. Your desired income at retirement is $50,000 per year. You will invest your retirement savings in IRAs and mutual fund annuities and hope to realize a rate of return at an average of 12 percent. How much do you need to save per month to realize your goal?

$50,000 (income per year) x 10 = $500,000 (A)

$500,000 (A) ÷ 1,000 = 500 (C)

500 © x $1.44 (B) = $720 (monthly savings needed)

* After-tax rates of return are used because most money should be in qualified retirement plans, IRAs, and mutual fund annuities, which are not taxed until after retirement. Assumed retirement age is sixty-five years.

TABLE 3
COLLEGE FUNDING WORK SHEET
HOW TO DECIDE ON A MONTHLY SAVINGS PLAN
FOR YOUR CHILD'S COLLEGE TUITION

Child's Age Now in Years	Monthly Savings Cost Per Thousand (B) at 10% Rate of Return*	Monthly Savings Cost Per Thousand (B) at 12% Rate of Return*	Amount Needed to Equal 1,000 Dollars at Time of High School Graduation (8% Inflation Assumed)
Newborn	$ 7.00	$ 5.54	$4,200
3	7.98	6.62	3,306
8	9.42	8.16	2,603
10	10.83	9.65	2,219
13	19.22	18.23	1,489
15	30.40	29.48	1,270

1) Estimate the total cost of a college education for your child, using today's dollars. _____ (A)

2) Referring to the above chart as to the age of your child, determine your monthly savings cost per thousand and the expected rate of return for the money you are saving toward college tuition. _____ (B)

3) Use the following formula to determine monthly savings needed.

_____ (A) ÷ 1,000 = _____ (C)

_____ © x _____ (B) = _____

(monthly savings needed)

Example: Your child is three years old. You estimate that it will cost $20,000 to put him/her through college. You will invest money toward his/her education and hope to realize a rate of return at an average of 12 percent. How much do you need to save per month to realize your goal?

$20,000 (A) ÷ 1,000 = 20 (C)

20 © x $6.62 (B) = $132.40 (monthly savings needed)

* After-tax rates of return are used because a mutual fund annuity, which is not taxed until the money is withdrawn, should be used for this investment.

CHAPTER 12

UNDERSTANDING WEALTH

By Ed Montgomery

THE MOST COMMON definition of wealth has catapulted many into an unending quest for security. This is unfortunate because this view equates wealth with only money. This is a great deception. Although money is certainly a part of wealth, money is not wealth in itself. The biblical view of wealth is provision through an unlimited supply. So wealth should be viewed in light of a present need, and money may not be that need. A need may consist of physical healing, peace of mind, direction, or purpose. This means a person can be poverty stricken—physically, mentally, or motivationally.

Many times we forget that God's ultimate will for us is complete wholeness in spirit, soul, and body. So financial wealth is not an end in itself. God dealt with man in the Old Testament to develop both physical and spiritual wholeness. Physical health, disciplined children, financial resources, and a good name were all considered as signs that Jehovah had His hand on an individual. A balanced view keeps financial wealth in its rightful place, not a supreme position.

I believe this is where the teaching of prosperity has caused ripples throughout the body of Christ for more than three decades. Many well-meaning people have taught and heard the "prosperity message" as representing an ultimate end. The same is true of salvation in some circles. Many get caught up in only bringing people to the place of being born again. This, of course, is primary and wonderful. Yet salvation is more than the new birth alone; it is also discipleship. To teach new birth alone and make it the primary goal robs the believer of spiritual maturity. God expects His children to grow up.

The same is true of prosperity. If we are only teaching financial well-being, believers will never grow up. So prosperity can't begin, nor should it end, with money. Money is just a fraction of the biblical teaching on prosperity.

As a matter of fact, some areas of financial poverty can be erased by a simple attitude adjustment. With the right attitude, God can prosper men and women in many areas. They may see immediate results through new job interviews, increased sales, and the increased energy level it takes to go into business. When Jesus healed He said, "Be made whole (complete)," (or, as He asked the cripple in John 5:6: "Wilt thou be made whole?" [KJV]).

Wealth is a whole-man principle because God's unlimited supply flows into every area of life. But I want to apply prosperity's concept of "unlimited supply." When we exhaust our search for an unlimited supply (wealth), we will ultimately come face to face with God. Isaiah 45:3 says: "And I will give thee the treasures of darkness, and hidden riches of secret places, that thou mayest know that I, the LORD, which call thee by thy name, am the God of Israel" (KJV).

Many years ago I watched a movie about the great Gold Rush of the nineteenth century. It told the story of men who packed up their families and headed for the hills of California to strike it rich. The majority of the people found little more than dreams. Since dreams didn't keep food on the table, they gave up and went back home. Some stayed, and every now and then would find a seemingly unlimited vein of gold. They called these veins "glory holes." I believe this is what God calls the "riches of secret places." God knows where the "glory holes" are!

Now I'm not advocating that you begin to dig around in your backyard. You may hit a water pipe, and that will cost you. What I am saying is there are vehicles of wealth that God will show you if you will learn how to plug in to Him! The Word says: "The secret things belong unto the LORD our God: but those things which are revealed belong unto us and to our children for ever, that we may do all the words of this law" (Deut. 29:29, KJV). In other words, the things of God belong to His children! So if God reveals a hidden source of wealth, it belongs to His people!

Pay special attention to the latter part of that verse "…that we may do all the words of this law [meaning spiritual laws]."

COVENANT

Many times we only view the Scriptures as God talking to us individually. And of course, we must receive the Bible as personal. However, we must also look at God's dealing with Israel from a historic point of view. As you study the historic accounts you will see that God was building a nation. And through that nation God planned to manifest Himself. Therefore, God's people had great responsibilities. One of those responsibilities involved providing for the continuance of the nation. To achieve this end, the people needed finances. God dealt with them through law, including the issue of money. But the end of the Law was always intended to instill a relationship through love. This love relationship is based on covenant.

The covenants God makes with His people are everlasting, without end, and actually translated "longer than forever." These covenants are not based on man's faithfulness to God; they're based on God's faithfulness to man….God made a blood covenant with Abraham, giving him and his descendants the land of Israel (Gen. 15:9–21). That covenant was renewed in Genesis 17:7–14 and again in Genesis 22. The covenant was extended to Isaac and to Jacob at Bethel. (See Genesis 28; Exodus 2:24; 6:3–5.)…

The concept of covenant is so important in the plan of God for man that it is mentioned 256 times in the Old Testament. Covenant is the soil in which every flower grows in Scripture. God does nothing, not ever, of importance without covenant. Evangelicals who teach that God broke covenant with the Jewish people can have absolutely no confidence that God will not break covenant with the Gentiles.

—JOHN HAGEE, *Earth's Final Moments*

Jehovah deals with His people based on covenant, which though unconditional in receiving forgiveness, was based on provisions of faithful obedience. God promised to provide for His people. In return His people were commanded to use their resources to support the extension of God's kingdom in the earth.

Paul writes of our New Testament covenant in Ephesians 4:28–29:

> Let him that stole steal no more: but rather let him labour, working with his hands the thing which is good, that he may have to give to him that needeth. Let no corrupt communication proceed out of your mouth, but that which is good to the use of edifying, that it may minister grace unto the hearers.
>
> —KJV

So God provides for those who are in covenant with Him, knowing that they will continue to further His will toward other men on the earth. We receive from God so we may have our own needs met, move the gospel, relieve the poor, and establish godly principles on the earth. This is the reason and purpose connected with biblical wealth.

MONEY

Although I have already given a covenant definition of wealth, the image of money probably still pops up. So let's not suppress it—let's deal with it.

Have you ever heard someone say, "I don't know what happens to my money; it just keeps getting away from me"? Well, contrary to what people think, money doesn't have legs. Money is an inanimate object that has no force of its own. It is amoral, neither good nor bad. Still, it does move.

As we move deeper into the twenty-first century, I see increasing amounts of money flowing into pornography, abortion, drug trafficking, and away from the poor and into the hands of the rich. This tells me that there is some force involved. But if money can flow into the cancers of our society, why can't it move into the healthy areas of life? First we must ask: "What is the force that causes money to flow?" The answer is: "People!" That's right—people! Whatever motivates people also motivates the direction in which money flows. If evil is the motivating force, then money will flow into the vehicles of evil. But if good is the motivating force, money can flow into the machinery that generates cures for sickness and comfort for the destitute.

So I think I've made my point. Money has no ears, legs, or arms. It doesn't hear us, it can't run or "get away" from us, and it certainly can't see us. Money doesn't see race, culture, or the color of one's skin. Racism and prejudice exist in our society, but there are those of every race who experience financial freedom—and financial bondage.

Education has some value, but we know there are rich people who have never finished high school or college. Hard work is commendable, but many people work hard all of their lives and stay continually poor. Nor is going to church any guarantee that you will prosper. If you violate certain principles, money won't flow in your direction. So, regardless of race, religion, or educational status, money will or won't flow, based on an individual's situation.

Why are the Jewish people loved permanently by God? Not just because "God is love" (1 John 4:8, NKJV). They are loved "for the patriarchs' sake." God made promises to Abraham, Isaac, and Jacob concerning the future of Israel and the Jewish people, and God will keep those promises. "It is impossible for God to lie" (Heb. 6:18, KJV)....

God has made promises to Abraham, Isaac, Jacob, and their descendants, and He must keep them to vindicate His own righteousness. Any Christian theology that teaches that God no longer loves the Jewish people or that God will no longer honor His covenant with them is false doctrine—it's simply not true, for it contradicts the teaching of the New Testament.

—JOHN HAGEE, *Earth's Final Moments*

When I speak of "money," I'm talking in terms of what other people will accept in exchange for something else. Things of value can't be viewed solely in terms of paper money. After all, the value of paper money fluctuates, going up and down like the price of oil. Why? Those who move it make it so. This fluctuation is caused by human beings. So never place complete trust in the value of paper money. Money is backed by a monetary standard that its movers adjust on any given day.

GOLD AND PRECIOUS STONES

Speaking of Adam and Eve's original environment, the Bible says:

The name of the first is Pison: that is it which compasseth
the whole land of Havilah, where there is gold; and the gold
of that land is good: there is bdellium and the onyx stone.

—GENESIS 2:11–12, KJV

Gold and precious stones are mentioned early in the Bible. The
minerals listed in the beginning were called "good" because they
were pure. There were no alloys or mixtures. It was God who
first placed value upon these minerals, and their original value
was purely aesthetic. These stones were valued for their beauty.
They reflected the beauty and glory of God.

Today gold and precious stones are valued for what they can
buy. Precious stones and minerals don't have intrinsic value,
because anything that has intrinsic value can't be affected by
external circumstances such as fire, flood, tricks, or schemes.
Therefore, gold is valuable because man puts value on it. God is
the only one who has intrinsic value, and He isn't moved by the
whims and changes of society.

Job 27:16–17 says:

Though he heap up silver as the dust, and prepare raiment
as the clay; he may prepare it, but the just shall put it on,
and the innocent shall divide the silver.

—KJV

When we plug our motivation into God—who has intrinsic
value—He is able to do great things through us with money. With
the proper motivation paper money in the hands of God's people
can be turned back into that which reflects the beauty and glory
of God. And what gives God glory? Good works that have the
life force of God as their motivation. Jesus said, "Let your light so
shine before men, that they may see your good works, and glo-
rify your Father which is in heaven" (Matt. 5:16, KJV).

When we take care of the poor and elderly, heal the sick,
liberate the drug addict, educate our children mentally and

spiritually, provide opportunities for work, and give purpose, meaning and direction to life, we make visible the glory of God! So remember, wealth is for wholeness, it is based on covenant, and can flow through trusting hands to do good works upon the earth. This is what Jesus meant when He preached:

> The Spirit of the Lord [is] upon Me, because He has anointed Me [the Anointed One, the Messiah] to preach the good news (the Gospel) to the poor; He has sent Me to announce release to the captives and recovery of sight to the blind, to send forth as delivered those who are oppressed [who are downtrodden, bruised, crushed, and broken down by calamity].
>
> —LUKE 4:18, AMP

CHAPTER 13

BREAKING THE SPIRIT OF POVERTY

By Ed Montgomery

IF THE SPIRIT of poverty has been oppressing your life, you must break the poverty cycle. I don't like to give formulas because all formulas don't work for all people. Every person has a different set of values and the conditions for receiving promises can vary with each individual. But there are some basic scriptural steps that everyone can use to walk out of poverty.

Step 1—Put poverty in its rightful position

First of all, you need to know that Jesus gave you something of inestimable value to empower you for a prosperous life.

> In my name shall they cast out devils...they shall lay hands on the sick and they shall recover.
> —MARK 16:17–18, KJV

Jesus gave us His name to destroy the works of Satan and overcome in life. This doesn't mean that using the name of Jesus will work as a magical word. On the contrary, when we use His name, we use His authority. Jesus has given us authority, but we must use it!

People are too often persuaded that they have no choices in life. It seems to many as if God has left them on this planet to fall victim to the vicious forces of this world's system. Religion has even taught us this. We have preached a message of "maybe and maybe not." But God is a God of specifics. He is specific about His Word, about the believers' life, and about His care for them.

I remember a boy named Arthur from elementary school who was a real bully. Everyone was afraid of Arthur—myself included. This boy was so threatening that I would hide behind trees or cross over to the other side of the street just to avoid him. But over time this became quite inconvenient. So I finally decided to put a stop to it, vowing to face Arthur the next time our paths crossed. When they did, we had a fight. To this day I'm not sure who won that fight, but from that moment on I never let the presence of Arthur dictate the course of my life. I never crossed another street that I didn't want to cross or delay myself by hiding behind a tree.

This is what authority does. When people recognize that the devil has been defeated, they no longer hide from him or the areas he has affected. When people discover their authority in Jesus's name, they no longer hide from creditors or feel ashamed of their present occupations. They realize that regardless of what their bank accounts say, the Word says they're more than conquerors. This encourages them to stop running and hiding.

It is here that the believer must trust the power of God to manifest itself in the sphere of conquering. Conquering what? The physical and spiritual results of poverty. There will be a learning curve and conflict here. When a person chooses to change habits that have been forged over the years, conflict follows.

I remember the first church I pastored. I had a wife, a daughter, and a son on the way. We had no medical insurance, nor any other source of income. On top of that, my starting salary was ninety dollars a week. That's right, a whopping ninety dollars a week! Yet, even with such a low income, the credit card companies approved my application. They *wanted* me to go into debt. So we used those cards to finance a baby bed, diapers, milk, clothes, and many other things that we needed. Before long we formed a habit of depending on plastic. Over the years this habit almost ruined us financially. Did I say almost? Well, it did ruin us. It took us several years to get out of credit card debt and to clear our names on various credit reports. For years that credit report followed us like a hound dog chasing a raccoon!

We eventually cleared everything up and started again. But I'll never forget that day when we first experienced the conquering power of Jesus Christ. That day Sandra and I sat down, took authority over our spending habits, fought the urge to use credit, and cut up our charge cards. Yes, we cut them up!

Now, I must be honest. I'm not a cut-up-all-the-credit-cards-and-never-use-one-for-the-rest-of-your-life fanatic. As a matter of fact, I still have one. Still, we never charge more than we are able to pay off each month. My point is, at the time we took our "cutting" action, our lifestyle exceeded our ability to pay for it. We had formed bad habits that had to be broken. Drastic circumstances demanded drastic measures. The credit cards weren't our problem—it was us! So we had to face facts, admit our mistake, and go in another direction.

What things control people and keep them in poverty? Is it credit cards? An overextended lifestyle? Too many financial fantasies? Habitual borrowing? Slothfulness in paying bills? Whatever is in control, the Word of God demands that believers break free. You can do this by totally committing to the truth of Jesus Christ. As the Savior said, "For whosoever will lose his life for my sake shall find it" (Matt. 16:25, KJV).

God knows the needs of His people, and promises to provide for them. However, His promises are contingent upon our complete abandonment unto Him.

> But seek ye first [or aim at] the kingdom of God, and his
> righteousness; and all these things shall be added unto you.
>
> —MATTHEW 6:33, KJV

I teach God's people to stand tall, fight, and declare: "Finances, debt, poverty, habits—I take my stand against you and refuse to let you take a stand against me, in Jesus's name! Jesus has given me victory over you, so go in Jesus's name!" This is where to start. I teach that poverty has a rightful position—right out of the lives of God's people!

Step 2—Acknowledge the source through giving

As some of you did, I grew up in the church, and vividly remember the atmosphere of the worship service during the offering. It was as if God had taken a fifteen-minute recess and walked out of the service! We must be reminded that giving is one of God's steps out of poverty.

Malachi 3:7 says: "Even from the days of your fathers ye are gone away from mine ordinances, and have not kept them. Return unto me, and I will return unto you, saith the LORD of hosts. But ye said, Wherein shall we return?" (KJV).

Malachi is describing the futile reality of a people who walked away from God. He is addressing people who rejected God's declared lifestyle and wound up in poverty. God was saying, "Return to me..." And how were they to return? Through giving, because verse 8 says: "Will a man rob God? Yet ye have robbed me. But ye say, Wherein have we robbed thee? In tithes and offerings" (KJV). Israel had robbed God, so reinstituting tithes and offerings represented the only way back. What? Tithes and offerings get us back to God? Yes, as far as national and individual prosperity are concerned. Remember Deuteronomy 8:18: "But thou shalt remember the LORD thy God: for it is he that giveth thee power to get wealth..." (KJV).

Notice the word *power*. It comes from the Hebrew word meaning "ability." So ability to make money comes from God.

Therefore, to deny God first access to our finances is to place other things in front of Him. The tithe and offering come first! From the top! Such giving acknowledges God as Lord of our finances. As Proverbs 3:9 says: "Honor the LORD with thy substance, and with the firstfruits of all thine increase" (KJV). When we do this, we walk under the system of blessing—not cursing.

> Ye are cursed with a curse: for ye have robbed me, even this whole nation. Bring ye all the tithes into the storehouse, that there may be meat in mine house, and prove me now herewith, saith the LORD of hosts, if I will not open you the windows of heaven, and pour you out a blessing, that there shall not be room enough to receive it.
>
> —MALACHI 3:9–10, KJV

When Russia and its allies march into Israel, they will be expecting to march out in victory. There will be no indication to them of what awaits them. They will have no awareness that they are making that march into Israel because God has put "hooks into [their] jaws," or that He is the one leading their armies, "all splendidly clothed, a great company with bucklers and shields, all of them handling swords" (Ezek. 38:4, NKJV).

Yet in Ezekiel 39 God has revealed the outcome of that confrontation with Israel, telling His prophet what He will do to Russia and its allies when they invade Israel in the near future:

"And I will turn thee back, and leave but the sixth part of thee, and will cause thee to come up from the north parts, and will bring thee upon the mountains of Israel" (Ezek. 39:2, KJV).

God declares He will exterminate all but one-sixth of the Russian axis of evil that invades Israel. Five out of six warriors in that great army will be killed. That's a death rate of 82 percent within just a few hours. It's no wonder the world will be stricken with shock and awe.

—JOHN HAGEE, *Earth's Final Moments*

But now you ask, "What if I can't afford to tithe?" I would remind you that God taught Israel about giving in the midst of their poverty. This means you can't afford not to tithe! You must have strength, ideas, ability, and energy to make money—which comes from God. So to withhold God's tithe is to bite the hand that feeds you. God is not against you; He is for you! But you must enthusiastically return to this principle to break free from the spirit of poverty and debt.

In recent years a great outcry about the financial resources of religious organizations has arisen, leading to many church leaders and pastors equivocating on the subject of tithes and offerings. I remember being challenged by a member of our congregation, who asked, "Pastor, do you believe that tithes and offerings are the way through which God provides for His people?"

"Yes, I do," I responded.

"Do you really believe that?" he said.

"Yes, I really do!"

Then this man said something I have never forgotten: "Then never be ashamed to teach it with assurance."

This is what church leaders and believers must avidly and unequivocally do. We must teach one another God's method of financial release with assurance.

The principles, concepts, and ideas I teach can help people to climb out of poverty—if they will apply them. Many can be used by the business community to make a lot of money. But along with financial prosperity comes the temptation to fall in love with financial success. The possibility of loving money is always there. This is why the apostle Paul warned: "The love of money is the root of all evil" (1 Tim. 6:10, MEV).

Notice that Paul said, the *love of money*—not money in and of itself—is the root of all evil. This is where I believe the tithe comes in. As long as God's people acknowledge God through the tithe, no matter how much money they make, they will retain an attitude of dependence on God.

Many have been confused about this. Some divide the tithe and spread it out among different ministries, family members, or various charities. But the Word is very specific: "Bring ye all the tithes into the storehouse." The storehouse is where the resources of God are kept. Where is the gathering of God's resources? The church, or the body of Christ on earth.

Are you in a local church? Is that church growing in faith and love? Are you receiving revelation from the Word of God through your church? Is your spirit being fed? Are you growing in ability, faith, and energy? Then give your tithe to the church where you are planted. What has helped you grow must continue to grow. And your tithes and offerings along with those of others in your local body will help the ministry expand and bless others.

Step 3—Put feet to your faith

Let me explain something very interesting about money. You acquire money through ideas, ability, and the exchange of work and energy. For example, if you work for a company at the rate of fifteen dollars an hour, eight hours a day, your income for one day will be one hundred twenty dollars. Now that equals the amount of ideas, ability, and work, you exchange for one day.

$$\text{Ideas} \times \text{Ability} \times \text{Work} = \text{Money}$$

Breaking the poverty spirit means bringing together the concepts of ideas and ability—the things that God puts inside of the believer. Even the unbeliever has this dynamic duo. But what causes these two powerful forces to activate is work. Yes, work. People must put feet to their faith. They must be encouraged to convert ideas and ability into action!

One of the greatest deceptions that has caused many people to become frustrated and to give up hope is the belief that their future depends on a job. Let me stress the importance of not merely looking for a job—but learning to look for work. There is a difference. Most people limit seeking a job to their particular field; or to their line of experience; or to a certain salary; or to their sphere of education. If they don't find a job in any of these four categories they give up and wind up in the unemployment line.

But work is anything that will yield a harvest—regardless of whether it meets a person's certain qualifications or not. Work isn't limited to a certain field of endeavor. It is just what it says—work!

Many times people will have to take a lower-paying position in order to temporarily make ends meet, and God will honor this. Take, for example, Ruth:

> And Ruth the Moabitess said unto Naomi, Let me now go to the field, and glean ears of corn after him in whose sight I shall find grace. And she said unto her, Go, my daughter. And she went, and came, and gleaned in the field after the reapers: and her hap was to light on a part of the field belonging unto Boaz, who was of the kindred of Elimelech.
>
> —RUTH 2:2–3, KJV

Ruth was unskilled, inexperienced, and unemployed. But to survive, she knew she had to work. Her first job: gleaning, the system that God provided to care for the poor and unemployed. It appears in Leviticus:

> And when ye reap the harvest of your land, thou shalt not wholly reap the corners of thy field, neither shalt thou gather the gleanings of thy harvest. And thou shalt not glean thy vineyard, neither shalt thou gather every grape of thy vineyard; thou shalt leave them for the poor and stranger: I am the LORD your God.
>
> —LEVITICUS 19:9–10, KJV

In this system when landowners reaped their harvest, they were forbidden to pick up the grain their harvesters left behind. It was to be left for the poor. What is significant to note here is that God didn't command the landowners to harvest all their crops and give a handout to the poor. No, He provided a system where the poor could work. That allowed them to experience the dignity and honor that comes from good, honest labor. Gleaning was backbreaking work. But if a person stuck to it, he or she could yield a minimum living. This was God's welfare system. The people had to work for it.

So if you're struggling with a spirit of poverty, let me encourage you to wake up, get up, stand up, dress up, and move out into the workforce. If you are embracing a "work-less" attitude, break free. Get up early tomorrow morning, wash your face, comb your hair, put on clean clothes, and go out trusting God to find work—work of any sort—until it leads to God's best.

I believe churches should consider providing certain chores and paying individuals for good honest work rather than freely supplying people from a benevolence fund. Of course there will be some exceptions, but the job of church leadership is more than to feed the belly. We must feed the spirit and the attitude of displaced people.

Men don't work to make money—money is a result of their work. And work is a stimulus to the dignity of the human being. God knew this. That's why God put Adam in the garden and put him to work. Adam was commanded to "keep" the garden or to "cultivate" it. So from the beginning of time, there has been a satisfaction to be gained from working with one's hands and seeing the fruit of one's labor.

Work was not a part of the Genesis 3 curse. But working independently of a relationship to the Creator will produce little fruit and few, if any, rewards. This is the curse. Work without ideas and ability produces little. But when a man works with the creativity and ability of God flowing through him, the true meaning of work is put in its proper, relational perspective. This I believe is the will of God: to work in relationship with our Creator. Do you see the connection?

When we give, we aren't just giving money; we're giving a portion of our time, ability, ideas, and energy. And since people exchange money for food, clothing, shelter, and the necessities of life, when they give, they're giving a portion of their lives. This is an important point. Money is a part of life.

Step 4—Look beyond your circumstances

There was a point in our lives when my wife, Sandra, and I couldn't see past poverty. We were surrounded by reminders of how poor we were. We grew up living in run-down neighborhoods, riding in old cars, and suffering unemployment because of the economy or racism. In the middle of all this we heard "religious" teachings that God wanted to make and keep you poor in order to relate to you. Can you imagine what kind of image we carried around? Not very encouraging, I guarantee you. If that is the kind of picture a person constantly receives, that is all they will achieve.

Ezekiel 39:6, "And I will send fire on Magog [Russia] and on those who live in security in the coastlands. Then shall they know that I am the LORD" (NKJV), suggests that judgment is coming not only to the invading Russian force but also on the headquarters of that power and upon all who support it or allowed this attack on Israel.

Notice the words: "I will send fire . . . on those who live in security in the coastlands." The word translated *coastlands* or *isle* in the Hebrew is *'iy*. The word was used by the ancients in the sense of *continents* today. It designated the great Gentile civilizations across the seas, which were usually settled most densely along the coastlands—just like America.

This fire Ezekiel sees coming to those living securely in the coastlands could be a direct judgment from God by hurricanes and tsunamis, or it could describe a nuclear war via an exchange of nuclear missiles. Could it be that America, who refuses to defend Israel from the Russian invasion, will experience nuclear warfare on our East and West Coasts?

—JOHN HAGEE, *Earth's Final Moments*

God's Word tells us, "Write the vision, and make it plain upon tables, that he may run that readeth it" (Hab. 2:2, KJV). People must have a picture or image of what they want to achieve and where they want to go. We don't think in words, we think in terms of pictures.

When Sandra and I first came to Houston we had about five hundred dollars in our pockets. We found a four-bedroom townhouse in a quiet section of town and paid for the first month's rent—which was five hundred dollars. That's all we had! Some will say we were foolish, presumptuous, and mismanaging our finances. I wouldn't suggest that anyone do this unless they are prepared to stand by their actions. Sandra and I had been building our faith for many years, but for the four years previous to our move, we had lived in undesirable conditions. I have probably seen every species of roach in North America. I refused to live like that any longer, so I decided to change our surroundings. It was time to get a new image!

Please don't misunderstand. I realize prosperity doesn't begin on the outside; it begins on the inside, within you. And I'm aware that you can live in a ghetto and be prosperous or that you can live in the most affluent part of town and be poor. But there does come a time when a person must change how they view things. If they're unemployed, they must see themselves employable and available to work. If people need a car, they need to start seeing themselves driving one. They need to start going to car dealerships and start talking cars. The greater the image, the closer that car will come to reality!

Now, when I start talking about image, some will say, "All that's fine, but I don't believe we need to have our heads in the sky." Why not? Ephesians 2:6 says, "And hath raised us up together, and made us sit together in heavenly places in Christ Jesus" (KJV). Jesus identified with tax collectors, prostitutes, fishermen, and the poorest of the poor. But Jesus never forgot who He was and where He came from. This was the secret of His authority. He knew Satan had no power over Him.

> And when the tempter came to him, he said, If thou be the Son of God, command that these stones be made bread.... And saith unto Him, If thou be the Son of God, cast thyself down: for it is written, He shall give his angels charge concerning thee: and in their hands they shall bear thee up, lest at any time thou dash thy foot against a stone.... And saith unto him, All these things will I give thee, if thou wilt fall down and worship me.
> —MATTHEW 4:3–9, KJV

When Satan tempted Jesus in the wilderness, he tried to pervert the image that Jesus had of Himself, His mission, and His ability. But Jesus didn't bow to Satan's perverted images. Instead, He declared the image He always confidently had:

> But he answered and said, It is written, Man shall not live by bread alone, but by every word that proceedeth out of the mouth of God.... Jesus said unto him, It is written again, Thou shalt not tempt the Lord thy God.... Then saith Jesus unto him, Get thee hence, Satan: for it is written, Thou shalt worship the Lord thy God, and him only shalt thou serve.
> —MATTHEW 4:4–10, KJV

Jesus identified with what the Word of God said. This is what God's people must do. They must see themselves as God sees them. God sees us as prosperous, having abundance, and giving to the needy. He sees us helping to spread the gospel of Jesus Christ and preaching the good news to the poor. So we must always teach people to see themselves as the Word of God sees them.

Step 5—Try different ideas

> His leaf also shall not wither; and whatsoever he doeth shall prosper.
>
> —PSALM 1:3, KJV

If we are ever going to prosper, we must do something! I want to handle this subject carefully, because I have a pressing reason for this. Most people who begin in this area normally think about going into business. Most think about part-time jobs, multilevel marketing, or other variations of these things. But the best place to start is where you are! Our first business venture is to maximize the job or career we're already working in, because prosperity always begins where you are...not where you aren't. So ask yourself these questions:

1. Do I get to work on time?

2. Am I performing my job equal to and beyond my employer's expectations?

3. Are there other positions available in my company I can aspire toward that will enable me to expand and grow?

4. Are there new and creative ideas that I can contribute to my company?

LOOKING FOR PROSPERITY? LOOK UNDER YOUR NOSE

God wants to prosper us right where we are. Many times the actual vehicles we need are right under our noses. So look for them and allow God to direct you as you achieve and grow.

Many have asked me, "What about multilevel marketing?" So I tell them that multilevel marketing can range from soap products to weight-loss programs. And I tell them that how well a person does in multilevel marketing depends on how well he or she can sell a product. Those who want to build a multilevel business must also be successful in recruiting others to duplicate their efforts. Therefore, in my opinion, multilevel marketing is a great opportunity to launch one into financial independence—that is, if you are diligent and willing to work.

Unfortunately many people are looking for instant financial success and violate basic principles. I know of hundreds who have bought and invested in starter kits, but they never start! The only people who prosper are the ones who sold them the kits. So whatever a person decides to do, he must do it!

In any business there are low times when the business seems to be failing. So if the motive is "quick money," you will soon become discouraged. This isn't the time to give up, but to press on! There is no "easy" way to make money. All things require diligence.

Still, I have a concern regarding some multilevel marketing businesses. I have been personally approached several times about a certain popular multilevel product. Marketing it involves attending a multitude of meetings and pep rallies, which can get in the way of church. I realize that any business takes time to build, but I noticed that the majority of those involved in this company were not just missing church, but also Bible classes and fellowship meetings. All in the name of "working their business."

Many justified this by saying their goal was to get rich so they could give to the ministry. My primary concern is that no believer should sacrifice teaching, fellowship, and worship for the purpose of making money. This is an unbalanced spiritual life. Yes, God does want us to prosper, but not at the expense of worship. Before we are called to be anything, we are called to be worshippers. God condones nothing at the expense of worship and fellowship. So always put God first, in worship and giving.

I have another concern. Throughout the years it has always amazed me how short-sighted we Christians can be! God is a God of creative innovation and unlimited ideas, yet we limit Him to two or three things. Notice what the Scriptures say: "Whatsoever he doeth shall prosper" (Ps. 1:3, KJV). This means exactly what it says—whatsoever! So God isn't limited to prospering through two or three specific product lines. Look at this particular scripture:

> And Esau took his wives, and his sons, and his daughters, and all the persons of his house, and his cattle, and all his beasts, and all his substance, which he had got in the land of Canaan; and went into the country from the face of his brother Jacob. For their riches were more than that they might dwell together; and the land wherein they were strangers could not bear them because of their cattle.
>
> —GENESIS 36:6–7, KJV

The Word says the land was not able to bear them. Even though some products have reached saturation levels, this doesn't mean God can't prosper us through them. It may take longer and pose greater challenges, but He can do it. This is where so many make mistakes. They are moved by testimonies of others who have made fortunes in a particular business and they assume the type of wealth gained by those who testify of it can only be found in that particular product. But remember, God can use anything!

It is time for believers to use their God-given creativity. There are products that have never reached certain states, gadgets that have never been invented, and services that have never been offered. So don't limit God or what He can do through people. As we search for new things, new ideas, new products, and new ways of making things work—God can receive great glory. Think about it!

Step 6—Find a Christ-centered church

Finally, I can't say enough about people settling into a good, solid, Christ-centered church. Too often people remain in churches because they grew up there, or their parents or grandparents attended there. Some attend because it's close to home or they're afraid to break out of certain traditional settings. All of these reasons are admirable, but they aren't always God's will. God's will is for His children to grow up in His Word—strong and healthy.

We shouldn't be afraid to question the belief structure of a particular church. The Word of God is well able to make things clear as to whether a church is spiritually alive or not. Some of the signs to look for in a stable congregation include:

1. The Bible is considered to be the ultimate and final authority.

2. The church has a vision for the future.

3. They believe in a well-balanced view of prosperity.

4. They teach the Lordship of Jesus Christ.

5. The love of God is shown through the actions of the membership.

6. They teach the Spirit-filled and Spirit-led life.

There are other things to look for, but these six are a good barometer. Also if someone you know is looking for a church with no problems—encourage them to stop looking! That animal doesn't exist! Where there are people, there will be problems. But problems can be overcome, and we have been called to be overcomers!

So encourage people to find a church and plant themselves there! As Psalms says: "Those that be planted in the house of the LORD shall flourish in the courts of our God" (Ps. 92:13, KJV).

God's people must learn how to deal with the multitude of problems that can arise as they deal with other people. Why? Because it's people who give to other people.

> Give, and it shall be given unto you; good measure, pressed down, and shaken together, and running over, shall men give into your bosom.
> —LUKE 6:38, KJV

So we must learn to deal with people. After all, that's who Jesus died for: sinful, flawed, sometimes madly irrational people. Then as we learn to develop everything God has put within us and put the Lord first, nothing can stop us from growing into God's promised prosperity and success.

The Word of God is alive with living principles that should motivate us to act. So let's do it. Let's take responsible action. For those who will obey His word, regardless of background or culture, God guarantees wholeness in every area of life, including financial success. Remember that management, not magic, is God's kingdom key!

CHAPTER 14

PRAYERS AND DECLARATIONS FOR PROVISION, BLESSING, PROTECTION, AND FAVOR

By John Eckhardt

HE SUBJECT OF blessing and prosperity has become quite controversial in the church. Certainly we want to be blessed and live the abundant life Christ died to give us. Yet we should never approach God as if He is a lottery or a slot machine—if you put in the right amount of prayer, praise, worship, faith, and good works, out comes your blessing. Sadly, that is the primary way some people see God. They simply get *beside themselves* when He doesn't come through for them the way they wanted.

However, blessing and prosperity are about more than money. According to *Strong's Complete Concordance of the Bible*, one Hebrew word for prosperity is *shalom*. We often associate the word *shalom* with *peace*, but the peace that Christ went to war for on the cross is a complete, whole kind of peace. Also according to *Strong's, shalom* is "completeness, soundness, welfare, and peace." It represents completeness in number and safety and soundness in your physical body. *Shalom* also covers relationships with God and with people.

God's thoughts concerning your peace and prosperity are much higher than you could imagine. It is His desire to bless and prosper you, and to give you His grace, favor, and protection. *Favor* means "grace"; "that which affords joy, pleasure, delight, sweetness, charm, loveliness"; and "good will, benefit, bounty, reward." If you look up the Hebrew and Greek definitions of *prosperity*, many of these words carry over into favor as well.

Favor is goodwill. This is God's kindness and benevolence given to those who love Him. Favor will release great blessings, including prosperity, health, opportunity, and advancement. The Bible records numerous examples of God's favor upon His people, causing them to experience many breakthroughs. Favor is God's loving-kindness.

Joseph experienced God's favor and went from prison to palace. God will do the same for you. He can change your circumstances in one day no matter where you are in life. This is when the favor of God is on your life.

Job was another blessed man who operated under God's full favor and blessing. In Job 10:12 he confessed that his life and favor were gifts from God: "Thou hast granted me life and favour, and thy visitation hath preserved my spirit" (KJV). Life and favor are gifts of God. We don't need luck. We need blessing. We need favor. We need the blessing of God. God desires to release new favor on your life. When you have God's favor and blessing, there is nothing in life that can hold you down.

When you walk in the favor and blessing of the Lord, others will recognize it. The favor and blessing of God on your life is one of the most powerful things God can release to you. As Jesus advised: "Seek ye first the kingdom of God, and his righteousness; and *all* these things shall be added unto you" (Matt. 6:33, KJV, emphasis added).

God says, "You don't need money. You need My favor." You

need His shalom—the full measure of peace—to operate in your life. This is your gift from Him if you are His child and are in covenant with Him. God blesses His people and rescues them. Just as He did with the Israelites, God loved you and chose you in spite of who you are and what you have done. You are elected by God. You were chosen before the foundation of the world. He chose you. It wasn't because of anything you've done. That is His favor!

God talks to the children of Israel in Ezekiel 16:1–14 about how He found them in a rejected state where they had been thrown away and no one wanted them. They were drowning in their own blood. But when God passed by, He said to them, "LIVE!" Then He blessed them and adorned them with jewels. God is saying this same thing to you. Maybe you were thrown away to die and had no chance at living. Maybe no one wanted you or you were not born with a silver spoon in your mouth. But when God looked upon you, He had mercy on you.

God will not only save you and wash you. He will also bless you, dress you up, put jewels on you, and beautify you. The grace and favor of God on your life will cause you to go into a place of prosperity. God not only will save you but will also multiply you and bless you.

When you learn confessions and prayers based on God's Word, they will activate His shalom over your life. Death and life are in the power of the tongue. We can choose blessing by choosing to live and speak correctly. God is ready to release new favor, blessing, prosperity, protection, and peace over you. It is His desire to give you good things. Now get ready to receive them.

ABUNDANCE AND PROSPERITY CONFESSIONS

I will prosper and be in health as my soul prospers.

I will not lack, for You are my shepherd, and I will not want (Ps. 23:1).

Lord, prosper me and let me have abundance.

Lord, You are El Shaddai, the God of more than enough; give me everything I need to fulfill my destiny, and let me have more than I need (Gen. 17).

Lord, You became poor that through Your poverty I might be rich.

Lord, let me not lack any good thing, for I delight myself in You.

Lord, give me the desires of my heart, for I seek You.

Lord, I put first Your kingdom and Your righteousness, and all things are added to me.

Lord, bless my coming in and my going out.

Lord, let me be blessed in the city and blessed in the field.

Lord, let me be blessed to be above and not beneath.

Lord, let me be blessed to be the head and not the tail.

Lord, let me be blessed with dominion and victory over the enemy.

Lord, let everything my hand touches be blessed.

Lord, let Your blessing overtake my life.

Lord, let Your favor bless my life.

Lord, command Your blessing on my storehouse.

Lord, command Your blessing, even life evermore, on my life.

Lord, let me have plenty of silver.

Lord, multiply Your grace in my life, and let me abound to every good work.

Lord, let me have abundance and not scarceness.

Lord, let there be no holes in my bag.

Let the windows of heaven be opened over my life and pour out a blessing I don't have room enough to receive. Lord, rebuke the devourer for my sake.

Lord, I seek You; cause me to prosper (2 Chron. 26:5).

Lord, speak over my life and let me prosper.

Lord, send Your angel and prosper my way (Gen. 24:40).

Lord, be with me and let me be a prosperous person (Gen. 39:2).

Let me have wisdom and prosperity (1 Kings 10:7).

Lord God of heaven, prosper me (Neh. 2:20).

Lord, take pleasure in my prosperity (Ps. 35:27).

Lord, send prosperity to my life (Ps. 118:25).

Let peace and prosperity be within my house (Ps. 122:7).

Let the gifts You have given me bring prosperity (Prov. 17:8).

Lord, You have called me; make my way prosperous (Isa. 48:15).

Lord, rule and reign over my life with prosperity (Jer. 23:5).

Lord, procure Your goodness and prosperity in my life (Jer. 33:9).

Lord, bless me, and let me not forget prosperity (Lam. 3:17).

Lord, let me prosper like Abraham (Gen. 24:35).

Lord, bless me and increase me like Abraham my father (Isa. 51:2).

Lord, let me prosper like Joseph (Gen. 39:2).

Lord, bless me like Asher, and let me dip my feet in oil (Deut. 33:24).

Lord, bless my house like the house of Obed-Edom (2 Sam. 6:12).

Lord, bless me and bring me into a wealthy place (Ps. 66:12).

Lord, give me power to get wealth (Deut. 8:18).

Lord, I am a giver; let wealth and riches be in my house (Ps. 112:3).

Lord, Your blessing makes rich, and You add no sorrow.

Lord, bless me with enough to eat, with plenty left (2 Chron. 31:10).

Lord, let me prosper like Daniel (Dan. 6:28).

Let ever journey I take be prosperous (Rom. 1:10).

Let every good seed I plant prosper (Zech. 8:12).

In the Book of Revelation John the Revelator declared that blood will flow up to the bridle of a horse for a space of sixteen hundred furlongs, which is approximately two hundred miles (Rev. 14:20). It will be a sea of human blood!

Look at a map of Israel. From the northern part of Israel to the southern point is about two hundred miles. The message? The battlefield will cover the nation of Israel!

It is beyond human comprehension to envision a sea of human blood drained from the veins of those who have followed Satan's plan to try to exterminate the Jewish people and prevent Jesus Christ from returning to Earth. Yet, in the theater of your mind, try to imagine the armies of the world, armed to the teeth, representing hundreds of millions of men eager to slaughter each other.

—JOHN HAGEE, *Earth's Final Moments*

PRAYERS FOR BONANZAS AND BREAKTHROUGHS

Lord, let my desire come, and let it be a tree of life (Prov. 13:12).

Let understanding be a wellspring of life for me (Prov. 16:22).

Lord, let Your fear give me life (blessing); let me be satisfied, and let me not be visited with evil (Prov. 19:23).

Lord, let humility and Your fear bring riches, life (blessing), and honor (Prov. 22:4).

I will live and not die, and will declare the work of the Lord.

Lord, show me the path of life; in Your presence is fullness of joy; at Your right hand are pleasures forevermore (Ps. 16:11).

Lord, give me life and length of days (Ps. 21:4).

Lord, give me Your favor, for in Your favor is life (Ps. 30:5).

For with You is the fountain of life; in Your light shall we see light (Ps. 36:9).

Let Your wisdom be a tree of life to me (Prov. 3:18).

Let Your words be life to my soul and grace to my neck (Prov. 3:22).

I will hold fast to instruction because it is my life (Prov. 4:13).

I have found wisdom, I have found life, and I obtain Your favor (Prov. 8:35).

Lord, You have redeemed my life from destruction. You crown me with loving-kindness and tender mercies (Ps. 103:4).

Let me enjoy the blessing of fruitfulness and multiplication (Gen. 1:22).

Let Your blessing come upon my family (Gen. 12:3).

I am blessed through Christ, the seed of Abraham (Gen. 22:18).

Let me be blessed greatly (Gen. 24:35).

Let those connected to me be blessed (Gen. 30:27).

Let me receive blessed advice (1 Sam. 25:33).

I walk not in the counsel of the ungodly, I stand not in the way of sinners, and I sit not in the seat of the scornful, but I delight in the law of the Lord, and I am blessed (Ps. 1).

Bless me, Lord, for I put my trust in You (Ps. 2:12).

Lord, I receive Your blessing for my transgression is forgiven and my sin is covered (Ps. 32:1).

Lord, bless me; I renounce and turn away from all guile, and iniquity is not imputed to me (Ps. 32:2).

Lord, bless me; You are my trust. I respect not the proud nor such as turn aside to lies (Ps. 40:4).

Lord, bless me; I consider the poor. Deliver me in the time of trouble, preserve me, and keep me alive. Bless me upon the earth, and deliver me not unto the will of my enemies (Ps. 41:1–2).

Lord, bless me for You have chosen me and caused me to approach unto You and dwell in Your courts, that I might be satisfied with the goodness of Your house (Ps. 65:4).

Lord, daily load me with benefits (Ps. 68:19).

Lord, bless me as I dwell in Your house and continue to praise You (Ps. 84:4).

Bless me, Lord; my strength is in You (Ps. 84:5).

Bless me, Lord, and let the light of Your countenance shine on me; I know the joyful sound (Ps. 89:15).

Let me be blessed by Your correction, and teach me out of Your Word (Ps. 94:12).

Bless me, Lord, and let me keep Your judgments and do righteousness at all times (Ps. 106:3).

Bless me, Lord, for I fear You and delight greatly in Your commandments (Ps. 112:1).

Bless me, Lord; I fear You and walk in Your ways (Ps. 128:1).

Bless me, Lord; I receive wisdom, watching daily at wisdom's gates, waiting at the posts of wisdom's doors (Prov. 8:34).

Lord, I have a bountiful (generous) eye; bless me (Prov. 22:9).

Bless me, Lord; I wait on You (Isa. 30:18).

I sow beside all waters; bless me, Lord (Isa. 32:20).

Bless me, Lord; I will not labor in vain or bring forth for trouble (Isa. 65:23).

Bless me, Lord. I trust in You, and my hope is in You (Jer. 17:7).

Let all nations call me blessed, and let me be a delightful land (Mal. 3:12).

Anoint me for breakthrough (Isa. 61).

Let me experience breakthroughs in every area of my life.

Let me break through all limitations and obstacles.

I will expand my tent, lengthen my cords, and strengthen my stakes, because I will experience breakthrough (Isa. 54).

The Lord my breaker goes before me (Mic. 2:13).

Let me break through in my finances.

Let me break through in relationships.

Let me break through in my health with healing.

Let me break through in my ministry.

Let me break through in my city.

Let me break through in my emotions.

Let me break through in my praise.

Let me break through in my prayer life.

Let me break through in my worship,

Let me break through in my revelation.

Let me break through in my career.

Let me break through in my giving.

Let me experience bonanzas in my life.

Let me experience Your "suddenlies," Lord.

Do a quick work in my life.

Let me experience great increase in a short period of time.

I believe in and confess BONANZAS for my life.

Let me find the vein of prosperity and experience bonanzas.

THE BLESSING THAT COMES FROM GIVING

The Bible teaches a simple message about being blessed to be a blessing. It is a cyclical law, much like sowing and reaping. In Christian circles it has been called the law of the harvest; in the world, karma; and in science, cause and effect: "What goes around comes around." "You get what you pay for." "You get out what you put in." "Whatever you sow, you will reap." Regardless of what man has tried to label it, this law of giving and receiving originated by the hand of God. It is not a hypothesis or theory. It is an ingrained law that applies to life on this earth and in heaven regardless of whether we are aware of it or not.

What you put out will be given back to you, and even more, you will receive in *proportion* to how you give. If you give (or sow) sparingly, you will receive (or reap) sparingly (2 Cor. 9:6).

If you want to receive the blessing of God, you have to be ready to give. You cannot expect to live a blessed life if all you do is receive, receive, receive. You will end up like the Dead Sea—becoming too salty and too toxic to support any kind of life. Blessed Christians are vibrant, fruitful, and able to give and sustain life. Everything around them is blessed. The spirit of death and staleness does not stay around them very long. Because they are blessed, they give blessing and in turn cause a flow of abundance.

Many churches today say that they have modeled themselves after the New Testament church, but the early church received and responded to the message of giving in a way that many today are reluctant to practice.

In 2 Corinthians 8:14–15 Paul encouraged the Corinthians to continue what they had always done, and that was for those with abundance to give to those who did not have so that no one would go without and that all would be blessed. He called this equality. In Acts 2:44–45 and Acts 4:32–33 it is also called having "all things in common" (MEV).

There was a living flow of blessings between the members of this church. Those who were blessed gave to those who were in need of a blessing. They did this willingly and cheerfully. (See 2 Corinthians 9:7–15.) In each of these instances the supernatural grace of God surrounded and blessed the givers and receivers. Giving wasn't a burden and the receivers were blessed enough to then become givers.

BLESSING AND FAVOR DECLARATIONS

Lord, You have granted me life and favor.

Lord, I thank You for life and life more abundantly.

I thank You for favor coming upon my life.

I believe that new life and new favor have been ordained for me.

Today I receive new life and new favor.

I believe favor is a gift of heaven.

I receive the gift of life—the gift of eternal life.

I receive the gift of favor and the gift of grace upon my life in the name of Jesus.

Thank You, Lord, for new grace and new favor, new prosperity and new blessing coming on my life.

I am the apple of God's eye.

I am one of God's favorites.

God favors me, loves me, and has chosen me from the foundation of the world to receive His grace and favor.

I receive extraordinary favor on my life in the name of Jesus!

GOD ESTABLISHED A COVENANT SO THAT HE COULD BLESS YOU

You must understand how much God wants to bless His people with peace. He is the God of peace. He is Jehovah Shalom. He is the Lord our prosperity. Israel couldn't see what was right in front of their eyes and missed it. So this blessing belongs to the new covenant church. We inherit the promise of shalom—prosperity, favor, peace, health, and safety—because we are the ones who, through the blood of Jesus, enter into a new covenant with God. What ancient Israel could not receive in the natural we receive in the spirit.

Covenant means faithfulness. Husband and wife have to be faithful to each other. Divorce comes into the picture because a covenant has been broken. Keep a covenant relationship with God. There is a huge advantage to doing this: blessing comes with covenant.

God does not just bless people for any reason. Being in covenant with God is a contract or a promise of His peace, safety, favor, protection, health, and prosperity. And God does not break His promises or go back on His word (Num. 23:19; Isa. 55:11).

Covenant with God is a mutual blessing. God gets a people, and we get God (Lev. 26:12). However, when God doesn't get a people, there is no need for the covenant. We cannot be God's own if we do not walk according to His covenant. He cannot claim us and put His name on us. Without Jesus, who is the Prince of Peace, shalom will never come. As Paul greeted the Romans: "To all who are in Rome, beloved of God, called to be saints: Grace to you and peace [prosperity, shalom] from God our Father and the Lord Jesus Christ" (Rom. 1:7, MEV).

Notice whom the peace goes to—not a physical people but those "called to be saints." The saints possess the kingdom of God. Are you a saint? This goes beyond being saved. The saints are the holy ones. It doesn't mean that you are perfect or don't make mistakes. It means that your lifestyle is holy. You don't *live* a sinful lifestyle. In the New Testament the saints walked in a level of holiness. They were not liars, drunkards, or whoremongers. They didn't mistreat people. If you are not a saint, you are not saved. The verse says, "Grace [*charis*, meaning favor] and peace to those who are called to be saints." If you are a saint, prosperity belongs to you, not because of anything you did or didn't do, but because of what Jesus did for us all on Calvary. That is the blood covenant. This is what brings you everything: provision, blessing, protection, and favor.

KINGDOM BLESSING CONFESSIONS

I am in the kingdom through faith in Christ, and I receive the blessings of the kingdom.

I receive the inheritance of the kingdom.

I receive the deliverance of the kingdom (Matt. 12:28).

I receive the healing of the kingdom (Matt. 10:1).

I receive and walk in the peace of the kingdom (Rom. 14:17).

I receive and walk in the joy of the kingdom (Rom. 14:17).

I receive and walk in the righteousness of the kingdom (Rom. 14:17).

I receive and walk in the power of the kingdom (Luke 9:1).

I receive and walk in the authority of the kingdom (Luke 9:1).

I receive understanding in the mysteries of the kingdom (Matt. 13).

I seek first the kingdom, and everything I need is added to me.

I reside and live in a blessed kingdom, and I receive the blessing of the King.

I receive the favor of the King.

I receive the protection and salvation of the King.

I will serve the King all the days of my life.

I am an ambassador of the King.

I have been translated from darkness into the kingdom of God's dear Son (Col. 1:13, KJV).

I am in the kingdom of light.

I receive the new wine and milk in the kingdom (Joel 3:18).

I enter into the rest of the kingdom.

ACTIVATING THE BLESSING OF SHALOM

Activating the blessings of God has everything to do with dwelling in the peace or shalom of God, which is an all-inclusive word that encompasses prosperity, safety, health, protection, fruitfulness, and abundance. According to the Hebrew definition, we can substitute the word *prosperity* with *shalom* (peace).

Religion has conditioned us to believe that life should be full of trouble and that one day we will go to heaven and then find peace. Well, peace is not only for heaven but also for the here and now on the earth. Your days should not be full of trouble. That doesn't mean trouble will not come, but you can stand up and tell trouble to go. You do not have to live a life of worry and anxiety. Peace is yours. Prosperity is yours. Even when trouble comes, it will not take away your peace.

The whole world is looking for peace. But there is only one way to peace, and that is through Jesus. He says, "I am the way…" (John 14:6, NKJV); "I am The-Lord-Is-Peace [Jehovah Shalom]" (Judg. 6:24). Having Jesus in your heart is the way of peace. No Jesus; no peace.

That's when prosperity comes; that is when blessing comes. Peace is what you have as a saint of God. You are also a peacemaker, and according to Matthew 5:9, you are blessed. You bring shalom wherever you go because Jesus is inside of you. You can change the whole atmosphere of a room, because the Prince of Peace lives inside of you. This is your covenant.

We stand on the brink of the best of times and the worst of times. It is the worst because man's rebelling against God, and His purpose for Israel makes it necessary for God to crush Israel's enemies.

Just before us is a nuclear countdown with Iran, followed by Ezekiel's war, and then the final battle—the Battle of Armageddon. The end of the world as we know it is rapidly approaching. Yet, through it all, God promises, "All Israel will be saved" (Rom. 11:26, NIV).

David's Son, King Jesus, will rule and reign for one thousand years in the Golden Age of Peace from Jerusalem. Rejoice and be exceedingly glad—the best is yet to be.

—John Hagee, *Earth's Final Moments*

The gospel is that Jesus Christ came and died so that you could experience the shalom of God. The chastisement—the price—of our peace was upon Him. He was beaten and crucified so we could have peace. All who believe and come under the rule of the Messiah can have peace.

You can have prosperity and live in safety, and all the evil beasts will be driven from your life. You will not be tormented by devils. You will have the blessing of God. It's the guarantee of His covenant of peace. It belongs to the saints of God. So no matter how bad the news gets, don't let the devil take your peace and your shalom away from you.

No matter what goes on, say, "Jehovah Shalom, You are my peace. You are my prosperity. You're the one who gives me shalom. I refuse to be tormented by the devil, to be vexed, harassed, oppressed, poor, or broke. I refuse to not have the peace of God because Jesus was chastised for my peace. I am a saint of God. I am in covenant. I have a right to peace. I can walk in that covenant. A thousand can fall at my side and ten thousand at my right hand, but it will not come nigh me, because I have a covenant of shalom."

Realize that it is not something coming one day. It's here, and it's yours. Jesus is the Prince of Peace. Do you have Jesus inside you? His peace is supernatural. It's already done. All you have to do is walk in faith, and it's yours. This is why Jesus came.

Peace is the kingdom of God. If you're not in the kingdom, you don't have shalom. If you call yourself a child of God, but you keep a lot of confusion, there's something wrong. A child of God is a peacemaker (Rom. 12:18; Heb. 12:14). Are you a peaceable person? Or do you like a mess? The church is intended by God to be a model of shalom to the world. When the world is struggling to find peace, where can they go? To whom can they turn? Where is the model for peace? Whom can the world look at to see a model for peace? Whom can they look at as a group of people from all different backgrounds—black and white, Jew and Gentile, coming together and living in peace because of the Prince of Peace? There is only one place that this happens—the church, where the wolf lies down with the lamb (Isa. 11:6; 65:25).

This is a picture that represents the coming of the Prince of Peace into the hearts of people, whereby they can love people whom they once hated. You can't be a child of God if you hate people. The church is the one place where we can show the world how to live in peace. That's our calling, and for it we will be blessed. Blessed are the *shalom* makers!

Sometimes we can get so caught up in strife that we begin to think that it's normal to have problems. But it's not. Command good days in your life to be at peace and full of blessing and prosperity. Speak blessing and prosperity over your neighbor, your troubled family member, and your coworkers.

Some don't think they are living unless it's hard. However, that is not what Jesus died for you to possess. You can enjoy a good life, especially when you "refrain your tongue from evil." Watch your mouth. Don't gossip, argue, fight, or add to confusion. And don't keep company with people who take part in that behavior. Seek peace. Peace is prosperity. You cannot have prosperity if you don't control your tongue. A blessed person is someone who knows how to guard his tongue.

Peace is one of the fruit of the Spirit (Gal. 5:22). As a child of God, confusion and strife vex you and don't agree with your spirit. You can't be around that. It is not *normal*. The church is to be God's community of shalom. As Paul said, "If it is possible, as much as depends on you, live peaceably with all men" (Rom. 12:18, NKJV).

Prosperous people are peaceful people. They are blessed. They have more than enough. They love life and see good days. They are citizens of the heavenly kingdom of God because they have been redeemed from the curses of sin and death.

PRAYERS FOR THE BLESSING OF SHALOM

Let me know the way of peace (Rom. 3:17).

May the God of peace be with me (Rom. 15:33).

Let mercy, peace, and love be multiplied to me (Jude 2).

Let peace come to me, my household, and all that I have (1 Sam. 25:6).

O Lord, lift Your countenance upon me and give me peace (Num. 6:26).

Thank You, Lord, for giving me Your covenant of peace (Num. 25:12).

I will depart from evil and do good; I will seek peace and pursue it (Ps. 34:14).

You have redeemed my soul in peace from the battle that was against me (Ps. 55:18).

Your law gives me great peace, and nothing causes me to stumble (Ps. 119:165).

Let peace be in my walls and prosperity within my palaces (Ps. 122:7).

Lord, You make peace in my borders and fill me with the finest wheat (Ps. 147:14).

I am spiritually minded; therefore life and peace are mine (Rom. 8:6).

Lord, You are not the author of confusion but of peace (1 Cor. 14:33).

You, O Lord, are my peace and have made me one with You (Eph. 2:14).

Let my household be counted worthy, so that Your peace will come upon it (Matt. 10:13).

The peace You give to me is not what the world gives; therefore my heart will not be troubled (John 14:27).

I will acquaint myself with You and be at peace, and good will come to me (Job 22:21).

Thank You, Lord, that You give me strength and peace (Ps. 29:11).

I pray that I will be meek and delight myself in the abundance of peace (Ps. 37:11).

Let me be like the one who is blameless and upright, for the future of that man is peace (Ps. 37:37).

Let my mind be stayed on You, and You will keep me in perfect peace because I trust in You (Isa. 26:3).

Lord, You establish peace for me (Isa. 26:12).

I will dwell in a peaceful habitation, in secure dwellings, and in quiet resting places (Isa. 32:18).

My children will be taught by the Lord, and their peace will be great (Isa. 54:13).

Let Your peace guard my heart and mind (Phil. 4:7).

Speak peace to me, God, and let me not turn back to folly (Ps. 85:8).

I pray that my ways will be pleasing to You, Lord, so that You will make even my enemies to be at peace with me (Prov. 16:7).

Your thoughts toward me are peace (Jer. 29:11).

Bring health and healing to me, O Lord, and reveal to me the abundance of peace and truth (Jer. 33:6).

I will pursue those things that make for peace (Rom. 14:19).

The God of peace will crush Satan under my feet (Rom. 16:20).

You have made a covenant of peace with me, and it is an everlasting covenant (Ezek. 37:26).

PRAYERS FOR THE BLESSING AND FAVOR OF GOD

Let me be well favored (Gen. 39:6).

Lord, show me mercy and give me favor (Gen. 39:21).

Give me favor in the sight of the world (Exod. 12:36).

Let me be satisfied with your favor like Naphtali (Deut. 33:23).

Let me have favor with You, Lord, and with men (1 Sam. 2:26).

Let me have favor with the king (1 Sam. 16:22).

Let me have great favor in the sight of the king (1 Kings 11:19).

Let me find favor like Esther (Esther 2:17).

Thou hast granted me life and favour, and Thy visitation hath preserved my spirit (Job 10:12, KJV).

I pray unto You, Lord, grant me favor (Job 33:26).

Bless me and surround me with favor like a shield (Ps. 5:12).

In Your favor is life (Ps. 30:5).

Make my mountain stand strong by Your favor (Ps. 30:7).

Because of Your favor, the enemy will not triumph over me (Ps. 41:11).

Through Your favor, I am brought back from captivity (Ps. 85:1).

Let my horn be exalted through Your favor (Ps. 89:17).

My set time of favor has come (Ps. 102:13).

I entreat Your favor with my whole heart (Ps. 119:58).

Let Your favor be as a cloud of the latter rain (Prov. 16:15).

Let Your favor be upon my life as the dew upon the grass (Prov. 19:12).

I choose Your loving favor rather than gold and silver (Prov. 22:1).

Let me be highly favored (Luke 1:28)

Show me Your marvelous loving-kindness (Ps. 17:7).

Remember Your mercy and loving-kindness in my life (Ps. 25:6).

Your loving-kindness is before my eyes (Ps. 26:3).

I receive Your excellent loving-kindness (Ps. 36:7).

Continue Your loving-kindness in my life (Ps. 36:10).

Let Your loving-kindness and Your truth continually preserve me (Ps. 40:11).

Command Your loving-kindness in the daytime (Ps. 42:8).

Your loving-kindness is good: turn unto me according to the multitude of Your tender mercies (Ps. 69:16).

Quicken me after Thy loving-kindness (Ps. 119:88, KJV).

Hear my voice according to Your loving-kindness (Ps. 119:149).

You have drawn me with Your loving-kindness (Jer. 32:18).

NOTES

CHAPTER 1
FINANCIAL FALLACIES THAT RULE THE WORLD

1. Wikipedia.org, "Thomas Robert Malthus," http://en.wikipedia.org/wiki/Thomas_Robert_Malthus (accessed February 23, 2015).

2. This paragraph was adapted from Phillip Longman, *The Empty Cradle* (New York: Basic Books, 2004), 133.

3. Sarah Gonzalez, "ERS Reports 10 Percent Increase in Corn Acres During Ethanol Decade," AgriPulse, http://www.agri-pulse.com/ERS_cropland_8192011.asp (accessed February 23, 2015).

4. *Science Daily*, "Biofuel Crops That Require Destroying Native Ecosystems Worsens Global Warming," February 11, 2008, http://www.sciencedaily.com/releases/2008/02/080207140809.htm (accessed February 23, 2015).

5. Michael B. McElroy, "The Ethanol Illusion," *Harvard Magazine*, November–December 2006, http://harvardmagazine.com/2006/11/the-ethanol-illusion.html (accessed February 23, 2015).

6. Roberta F. Mann and Mona L. Hymel, "Moonshine to Motorfuel: Tax Incentives for Fuel Ethanol," *Duke Environmental Law & Policy Forum* 19 (2008), 43.

7. Mark Steyn, "Chickenfeedhawks: Global Warm-Mongering," *Greenie Watch*, http://antigreen.blogspot.com/2008_05_01_archive.html (accessed February 23, 2015).

8. *China Daily*, "Moving Millions Rebuild a Nation," October 2, 2004, http://www.china.org.cn/english/China/108570.htm (accessed February 23, 2015).

9. Joel K. Bourne Jr., "The Global Food Crisis," *National Geographic*, June 2009, http://ngm.nationalgeographic.com/print/2009/06/cheap-food/bourne-text (accessed February 23, 2015).

10. Ibid.

11. Ibid.

12. For more information about the Club of Rome, http://www.cluboframe.org/eng/home/.

13. Joint Economic Committee of the United States Congress, "The U.S. Economy at the Beginning and End of the 20th Century," December 1999.

14. Paul Ehrlich, *The Population Bomb* (New York: Ballantine Books, 1971).

15. David Cork, *The Pig in the Python* (Toronto: Stoddart Books, 1996).

16. Urban Institute, "The U.S. Population Is Aging," http://www.urban.org/retirement_policy/agingpopulation.cfm (accessed February 24, 2015).

17. Francis Bator, "LBJ and the Vietnam/Great Society Connection," *American Academy of Arts and Sciences*, 2007, http://www.amacad.org/publications/BatorWeb.pdf (accessed February 24, 2015).

18. Information in this paragraph was obtained from a 2002 CNBC Broadcast.

19. Information in this table was obtained from The Heritage Foundation.

20. PBS, "Timeline: The Pill," http://www.pbs.org/wgbh/amex/pill/timeline/timeline2.html (accessed February 24, 2015).

21. History.com, "This Day in History: January 23, 1973," http://www.history.com/this-day-in-history/supreme-court-legalizes-abortion (accessed February 24, 2015).

22. Milton Friedman, "Famous Quotes by Milton Friedman," *Book of Famous Quotes*, http://www.famous-quotes.com/author.php?aid=2647 (accessed February 24, 2015).

23. Robert Barro and Xavier Sala-i-Martin, *Economic Growth* (Cambridge, MA: The MIT Press, 2003).

24. Social Security Online, "Status of the Social Security and Medicare Programs," http://www.ssa.gov/OACT/TRSUM/index.html (accessed February 24, 2015).

25. William H. Gross, "'Bon' or 'Non' Appétit?" PIMCO, July 2009, http://www.pimco.com/en/insights/pages/investment%20outlook%20july%202009%20gross%20appetit.aspx (accessed April 7, 2015).

26. For more information about the decade of deflation in Japan during the late 1980s and early 1990s, see Gary Saxonhouse, *Japan's Lost Decade* (Hoboken, NJ: Wiley-Blackwell, 2004).

27. William Overholt, "Asia's Continuing Crisis," http://overholtgroup.com/media/Articles-Asia-General/Asias-Continuing-Crisis-Text.pdf (accessed February 24, 2015).

28. Dave Manuel, "Nikkei 225 Hit All-Time High of 38,957.00 on December 29th, 1989," April 16, 2009, https://tinyurl.com/coof2w (accessed February 24, 2015).

29. *World Bank Development Indicators*, "Global Income Per Capita," http://web.worldbank.org/WBSITE/EXTERNAL/DATASTAT ISTICS/0,,contentMDK:21298138~pagePK:64133150~piPK:64133175 ~theSitePK:239419,00.html (accessed July 15, 2009).

30. Money Management Solutions, "How to Become a Millionaire During the Depression," June 11, 2008, http://moneymgmtsolutions .com/blog/debt-consolidation/how-to-become-a-millionaire-during -the-depression/ (accessed February 24, 2015).

CHAPTER 2
BRACING FOR THE BIG CHILL

1. Neil Irwin, "Why the Housing Market Is Still Stalling the Economy," *New York Times*, April 24, 2014, http://www.nytimes.com/ 2014/04/27/upshot/the-housing-market-is-still-holding-back-the -economy-heres-why.html?_r=1&abt=0002&abg=1 (accessed February 24, 2015.

2. *Gary Shilling Insight*, July 2009.

3. T2 Partners LLC, "An Overview of the Housing Crisis and Why There Is More Pain to Come."

4. Ibid.

5. Ibid.

6. Carmen M. Reinhart and Kenneth S. Rogoff, "The Aftermath of Financial Crises," December 19, 2008, http://www.economics.harvard .edu/files/faculty/51_Aftermath.pdf (accessed February 24, 2015).

7. Federal Reserve Flow of Funds Accounts of the United States, IMF Global Financial Security Report, October 2008, Goldman Sachs Global Economics Paper No. 177, FDIC Quarterly Banking Profile, OFHEO, S&P Leverage Commentary and Data, T2 Partners estimates.

8. James Gruber, "Japan's 20-Year Deflationary Spiral Is About to End," Forbes.com, April 27, 2014, http://www.forbes.com/sites/ jamesgruber/2014/04/27/japan-deflation-to-end (accessed March 26, 2015).

9. Kimberly Amadeo, "Savings and Loans Crisis," About.com: US Economy, http://useconomy.about.com/od/grossdomesticproduct/ p/89_Bank_Crisis.htm (accessed February 25, 2015).

10. This information was obtained from Cornerstone Financial Services.

11. Justin Wolfers, "The Fed Has Not Stopped Trying to Stimulate the Economy," *New York Times*, October 29, 2014, http://www .nytimes.com/2014/10/30/upshot/the-fed-has-not-stopped-trying-to

-stimulate-the-economy.html?rref=upshot&abt=0002&abg=1&_r=0 (accessed February 25, 2015).

12. Harry S. Dent, July 2009.

13. From an interview on CNBC, cited by Gabriel Madway, "Paulson: Subprime Mortgage Fallout 'Largely Contained,'" Market Watch, March 13, 2007, http://www.marketwatch.com/story/paulson-subprime -mortgage-fallout-largely-contained (accessed February 25, 2015).

14. From a speech given to Congress, cited by Jeannine Aversa, "Bernanke Says No Recession in Sight," *Seattle Times*, March 28, 2007, http://seattletimes.nwsource.com/html/businesstechnology/ 2003639710_webbernanke28.html (accessed February 25, 2015).

15. In a speech to The Committee of 100 in New York, cited in "Subprime Woes Likely Contained: Treasury's Paulson," Reuters, April 20, 2007, http://www.reuters.com/article/gc06/ idUSWBT00686520070420 (accessed February 25, 2015); Wanfeng Zhou, "Paulson Urges China to Make Yuan More Flexible," Market Watch, April 20, 2007, http://www.marketwatch.com/story/treasurys -paulson-urges-china-to-make-yuan-more-flexible (accessed February 25, 2015).

16. From a speech before the Federal Reserve Bank of Chicago, cited in Evelyn M. Rusli, "Bernanke Believes Housing Mess Contained," May 17, 2007, Forbes.com, http://www.forbes.com/2007/05/17/ bernanke-subprime-speech-markets-equity-cx_er_0516markets02 .html (accessed February 24, 2015).

17. From a conversation with President George W. Bush, cited in Marc Gunther, "Paulson to the Rescue," CNN Money, September 16, 2007, http://money.cnn.com/2008/09/13/news/newsmakers/gunther_ paulson.fortune/index2.htm (accessed July 16, 2009).

18. From an interview in Washington, cited in Kevin Carmichael and Peter Cook, "Paulson Says Subprime Rout Doesn't Threaten Economy," Bloomberg.com, July 26, 2007, http://www.bloomberg .com/apps/news?pid=20601087&sid=aMy9XODlJOnc&refer=home (accessed February 25, 2015).

19. From the transcript of Secretary Paulson's Press Roundtable in Beijing, China, on August 1, 2007, Press Room, U.S. Department of the Treasury, http://www.treasury.gov/press-center/press-releases/ Pages/hp525.aspx (accessed February 25, 2015).

20. From comments presented before the Senate Banking Committee about the economy, cited in Chris Isidore, "Paulson, Bernanke: Slow Growth Ahead," CNNMoney.com, February 14, 2008,

http://money.cnn.com/2008/02/14/news/economy/bernanke_paulson/ (accessed February 24, 2015).

21. From comments presented to the Senate Banking Committee, cited in Alistair Bull, "US Banks Should Seek More Capital—Bernanke," Reuters, February 28, 2008, http://www.reuters.com/article/2008/02/28/sppage012-n28573663-oisbn-idUSN2857366320080228 (accessed February 25, 2015).

22. Michael M. Phillips and Damian Paletta, "Paulson Sees Credit Crisis Waning," *Wall Street Journal*, May 7, 2008, http://www.wsj.com/articles/SB121011652297872261 (accessed February 25, 2015).

23. From a speech to business executives in Washington, cited in "Markets Calmer, Says Treasury Secretary," CBSNews.com, May 16, 2008, http://www.cbsnews.com/stories/2008/05/16/business/main4103698.shtml?source=RSSattr=Business_4103698 (accessed February 25, 2015).

24. From remarks to the Boston Federal Reserve's 52nd annual economic conference in Massachusetts, cited in Craig Torres and Scott Lanman, "Bernanke Says Risk of 'Substantial Downturn' Has Diminished," Bloomberg.com, June 9, 2008, http://www.bloomberg.com/apps/news?pid=newsarchive&sid=aH6u3wsqwMFM&refer=worldwide (accessed February 25, 2015).

25. From an interview on *Face the Nation* on CBS, July 21, 2008, cited in "Paulson: U.S. Banking System Fundamentally Sound," Reuters, http://www.cnbc.com/id/25764545/ (accessed February 25, 2015).

26. Reuters, "Excerpts From Geithner's Speech on Bank Plan," February 10, 2009, http://www.reuters.com/article/ousiv/idUSTRE5194C920090210?sp=true (accessed February 25, 2015).

27. From a transcript of President Obama's news conference on March 24, 2009, http://www.nytimes.com/2009/03/24/us/politics/24text-obama.html (accessed February 25, 2015).

28. From remarks to the Economic Club of Washington, cited in Corbett B. Daly and David Lawder, "Summers Says Economic 'Free-Fall' to End Soon," Reuters, April 10, 2009, http://www.reuters.com/article/ousiv/idUSTRE53859920090409 (accessed February 25, 2015).

29. From an address to students and faculty of Morehouse College in Atlanta, cited in Ben Rooney, "Bernanke Sees 'Signs' Decline Is Easing," CNNMoney.com, April 14, 2009, http://money.cnn.com/2009/04/14/news/economy/Bernanke/index.htm (accessed February 25, 2015).

CHAPTER 3
WEATHERING THE FINANCIAL STORM

1. Adapted from Jerry and Ramona Tuma, *Smart Money* (Dallas, TX: Cornerstone Financial Services, 2003), 187–209.

2. Thomas J. Stanley and William D. Danko, *The Millionaire Next Door* (New York: Pocket Books, 1999).

3. Adapted from the summary for Stanley and Danko, *The Millionary Next Door.*

4. Ibid., 3–4.

5. Thomas J. Stanley, *The Millionaire Mind* (Kansas City, MO: Andrews McMeel Publishing, 2001).

6. Wikipedia, "Buy and Hold," http://en.wikipedia.org/wiki/Buy_and_hold (accessed February 25, 2015).

7. "Absolute Return Investing," Absolute Investment Advisers, http://www.absoluteadvisers.com/ari.htm (accessed July 22, 2009).

8. James Stockdale, cited in Jim Collins, *Good to Great* (New York: HarperCollins, 2001).

9. Christian Tondo, "Effects of the Dot-com Crash on Pensions in Industrialized Countries," http://www.watsonwyatt.com/pubs/directions/media/2009_EU_12059_Directions_04_dot-com_web.pdf (accessed July 22, 2009).

10. Jeremy Siegel, *The Future for Investors* (New York: Crown Business, 1st edition, 2005).

11. Jeremy Siegel, *Stocks for the Long Run* (Columbus, OH: McGraw-Hill, 2002).

12. Keith Timimi, "Reserve Currency: China Says Move Beyond the US Dollar, Calls for a New Super-Sovereign Currency," *Economy Watch*, June 29, 2009, http://www.economywatch.com/economy-business-and-finance-news/reserve-currency-china-says-move-beyond-the-US-dollar-calls-for-a-new-super-sov-currency.html (accessed February 25, 2015).

13. *Energy Business Reports*, "Growing Energy Demand in India and China," October 2007, http://www.researchandmarkets.com/reports/563478 (accessed July 23, 2009).

14. Martin Hutchinson, "Auto Industry Moves to India and China," Money Morning, http://www.moneymorning.com/2008/01/14/auto-industry-moves-to-india-and-china (accessed February 24, 2015).

15. Electronic Product News, "Infrastructure in China," http://www.epn-online.com/page/37042/infrastructure-in-china.html (accessed July 23, 2009).

16. InfiBeam, "Tata Nano Geared up for Grand Launch," http://news.infibeam.com/blog/news/2009/02/25/tata_nano_geared_up_for_grand_launch.html (accessed July 23, 2009).

17. Information in this table was obtained from US Energy Information Agency.

18. Information in this table was obtained from US Energy Information Agency.

19. As quoted in Timothy L. Hall, Religion in America (New York: Facts on File Inc., 2007), 41. Viewed at Google Books.

CHAPTER 4
GROWING YOUR WAY TO PROSPERITY

1. National Priorities Project, "Federal Spending: Where Does the Money Go," https://www.nationalpriorities.org/budget-basics/federal-budget-101/spending/ (accessed February 25, 2015).

2. Hoisington Investment Management Company, *Quarterly Review and Outlook*, Second Quarter 2009.

3. Harry S. Dent, "The Right Tool for Predicting and Capitalizing on Today's Market Opportunities," *HS Dent Economic Forecast*, August 8, 2008, http://www.hsdent.com/economicforecast/?gclid=CMTtkaS55JsCFU1M5QodHgObAw (accessed July 20, 2009).

4. Dennis Nishi, "How Buck Knives Decided to Move HQ," *Wall Street Journal*, July 14, 2009, http://www.wsj.com/articles/SB124760533703141285 (accessed February 26, 2015).

5. Kim Web, "Luxury Tax Rides Off Into the Sunset," *Kiplinger Report*, November 15, 2002, http://www.highbeam.com/doc/1G1-123379236.html (accessed July 20, 2009).

6. Herb Meyer, "What in the World Is Going On? A Global Intelligence Briefing for CEOs," http://www.nnseek.com/e/uk.local.manchester/herb_meyer_at_the_world_economic_forum_in_davos_sw_118690975m.html (accessed February 24, 2015).

7. Jim Collins and Jerry Porras, *Built to Last* (New York: HarperCollins, 2004).

8. Jim Collins, *Good to Great* (New York: HarperCollins, 2001).

9. Ibid., 86.

10. There are numerous accounts of the Battle of the Alamo available online. You may see one account at http://www.britannica.com/EBchecked/topic/12135/Alamo.

11. William Barret Travis, "To the President of the Convention, March 3, 1836," *William Barret Travis—Alamo Letters*, http://www .ntanet.net/travis.html (accessed February 26, 2015).

12. Kennedy Hickman, "Texas Revolution: Battle of San Jacinto," About.com: Military History, http://militaryhistory.about.com/od/ battleswars1800s/p/sanjacinto.htm (accessed February 26, 2015).

13. George Santayana, "The Life of Reason, Volume 1 (1905)," The Quotations Page, http://www.quotationspage.com/quote/2042.html (accessed February 26, 2015).

14. Alexander Fraser Tyler [Tytler], "Cycle of Democracy (1770)," Famous Quotes, http://www.famousquotessite.com/famous-quotes -6934-alexander-fraser-tyler-cycle-of-democracy-1770.html (accessed February 26, 2015).

CHAPTER 7
ACTIVATE THE BLESSINGS OF GOD

1. C. Thomas Anderson, *Becoming a Millionaire God's Way* (Nashville, TN: FaithWords, 2008), 30–31.

2. Theo Wolmarans, *How to Recognize the Voice of God* (Bonaero Park, S. Africa: Theo and Beverley Christian Enterprises, 2009), 165.

3. Edward K. Rowell, ed., *1001 Quotes, Illustrations and Humorous Stories* (Grand Rapids, MI: Baker Books, 2008), 42.

4. Jentezen Franklin, *Believe That You Can* (Lake Mary, FL: Charisma House, 2008), 46.

CHAPTER 8
HARNESSING THE WISDOM OF GOD

1. John MacArthur, *The MacArthur Bible Commentary* (Nashville, TN: Thomas Nelson, 2005), 1240, "Here it symbolizes Israel" (cf. Ps. 80:8–16; Isa. 5:1; Jer. 2:21).

2. Phil Pringle, *Leadership Excellence* (Dee Why, Australia: Pax Ministries Pty Ltd., 2005), 172.

3. Charles Spurgeon, *The Soul Winner* (New Kensington, PA: Whitaker House, 1995), 9.

4. Ryan Mauro, "Paul Williams Details 'American Hiroshima,'" World Net Daily, September 3, 2005, http://www.wnd.com/2005/09/ 32145/ (accessed February 27, 2015).

5. Henry Cloud, *Necessary Endings* (New York: HarperBusiness, 2011).

6. Ibid.

7. Ibid.

8. Ibid.

9. John C. Maxwell, *There's No Such Thing as Business Ethics* (Nashville, TN: CenterStreet, 2003).

CHAPTER 9
THE REALITY OF POVERTY IN OUR WORLD

1. The World Bank, "Inequality in Focus, October 2013: Analyzing the World Bank's Goal of Achieving 'Shared Prosperity,'" http://www .worldbank.org/en/topic/poverty/publication/inequality-in-focus -october-2013 (accessed February 27, 2015).

2. Branko Milanovic, "True World Income Distribution," World Bank Publications, 1999, 52.

3. A World Bank Policy Research Report, *Globalization, Growth and Poverty: Building an Inclusive World Economy* (New York: World Bank and Oxford University Press, 2002), https://tinyurl.com/kklgx45 (accessed February 27, 2015).

4. Country Studies, "South Africa," http://countrystudies.us/south -africa/66.htm (accessed February 27, 2015).

5. The World Factbook, "Country Comparison: Crude Oil – Production," Central Intelligence Agency, https://www.cia.gov/library/ publications/the-world-factbook/rankorder/2241rank.html (accessed February 27, 2015).

6. As quoted by Colin Powell, "Remarks at the Development, Democracy and Security Bretton Woods Committee Conference," September 30, 2004, U.S. Department of State Archive, http://2001 -2009.state.gov/secretary/former/powell/remarks/36649.htm (accessed March 1, 2015).

7. United Nations Children's Fund, *The State of the World's Children, 1999,* cited in John C. Holveck et al., "Prevention, Control, and Elimination of Neglected Diseases in the Americas: Pathways to Integrated, Interprogrammatic, Inter-sectoral Action for Health and Development," *BMC Public Health 2007,* January 17, 2007, http://www .biomedcentral.com/content/pdf/1471-2458-7-6.pdf (accessed March 1, 2015).

8. Unicef, *Levels & Trends in Child Mortality 2014,* http://www unicef.org/media/files/Levels_and_Trends_in_Child_Mortality_2014 .pdf (accessed March 1, 2015).

9. Peter S. Goodman, "Big Shift in China's Oil Policy," *Washington Post*, July 13, 2005, http://www.washingtonpost.com/wp-dyn/content/article/2005/07/12/AR2005071201546.html (accessed March 1, 2015).

10. The World Bank, "Poverty Overview," October 7, 2014, http://www.worldbank.org/en/topic/poverty/overview (accessed March 1, 2015).

11. Milanovic, "True World Income Distribution."

12. United Nations Children's Fund, *The State of the World's Children, 1999.*

CHAPTER 10
FINANCIAL FREEDOM AND THE BASIC LAWS OF MONEY

1. Chris Joyner, "Bank Robberies Up Around USA," *USA Today*, http://www.usatoday.com/news/nation/2008-06-15-bankrobberies_N.htm (accessed March 1, 2015).

2. FBI, "Bank Crime Statistics 2008," http://www.fbi.gov/stats-services/publications/bank-crime-statistics-2008/bank-crime-statistics-2008-final (accessed March 1, 2015).

3. "Bank Crime Statistics 2011," http://www.fbi.gov/stats-services/publications/bank-crime-statistics-2011/bank-crime-statistics-2011 (accessed March 1, 2015).

4. "56,662,169 Abortions in America Since Roe vs. Wade in 1973," Life News, January 12, 2014, http://www.lifenews.com/2014/01/12/56662169-abortions-in-america-since-roe-vs-wade-in-1973/ (accessed March 1, 2015).

CHAPTER 11
THE LAND MINE OF FAILING TO PLAN

1. Emily Brandon, "Poverty Increasing Among Retirees," *U.S. News and World Report*, May 21, 2012, http://money.usnews.com/money/retirement/articles/2012/05/21/poverty-increasing-among-retirees (accessed March 1, 2015).

SUBSCRIBE TODAY

Exclusive content

Delivered directly to you

Stay current

Update others

CHARISMA MEDIA

FREE NEWSLETTERS
TO EMPOWER YOUR LIFE

PROPHETIC INSIGHT
Receive Prophetic messages from respected leaders in the body of Christ delivered straight to your inbox shortly after they are given.

STANDING WITH ISRAEL
Do you have a heart for God or Israel? Stay informed of Israel-related news and Christian Zionist activities. News, articles and information from around the world as it pertains to our friends in Israel.

CHARISMA MAGAZINE
Stay up-to-date with a recap of top-trending articles, Christian teachings, entertainment reviews, videos and more from your favorite magazine and website.

CHARISMA NEWS DAILY
Tired of the liberal media? Get the latest breaking Christian news you need to know about as soon as it happens from the editors of *Charisma*.

SIGN UP AT: nl.charismamag.com